Standard Work for Lean Healthcare

Lean Tools for Healthcare Series

Series Editor: Thomas L. Jackson

PUBLISHED

5S for Healthcare

Standard Work for Lean Healthcare

FORTHCOMING

Just-in-Time for Healthcare

Kaizen Workshops for Lean Healthcare

Mistake Proofing for Lean Healthcare

Standard Work for Lean Healthcare

Rona Consulting Group & Productivity Press

Thomas L. Jackson, Editor

CRC Press
Taylor & Francis Group
Boca Raton   London   New York

CRC Press is an imprint of the
Taylor & Francis Group, an **informa** business

A PRODUCTIVITY PRESS BOOK

CRC Press
Taylor & Francis Group
6000 Broken Sound Parkway NW, Suite 300
Boca Raton, FL 33487-2742

Version Date: 20110705

International Standard Book Number: 978-1-4398-3741-2 (Paperback)

Visit the Taylor & Francis Web site at
http://www.taylorandfrancis.com

and the CRC Press Web site at
http://www.crcpress.com

Contents

Preface

Any healthcare organization that is a leader in today's marketplace for healthcare services understands the importance of basic standards—rules for what is acceptable and what is not—in practices, processes, service quality, patient safety, employee policies, and so on. Standard work characterizes such an organization, in both its management activities and daily operations. The organization that practices standardization has processes for creating standards and standard work, for communicating them clearly, for maintaining and adhering to them, and for encouraging their continual examination and improvement.

In healthcare operations, standard work is a key element in eliminating process waste, ensuring patient safety, improving flow, and achieving balanced and synchronous production of healthcare services. *Standard Work for Lean Healthcare* has been written specifically to help your organization apply standards, standardization, and standard work to its healthcare processes. However, throughout the text there is also guidance for how management can support these initiatives.

The information in *Standard Work for Lean Healthcare* is presented in a highly organized and easy-to-assimilate format. There are numerous illustrations to reinforce the text. Margin assists call your attention to key points and other important features. And throughout the book you are asked to reflect on questions that will help you apply these concepts and techniques to your own workplace. Each chapter has a summary for quick review.

Chapter 1 helps you get started by suggesting strategies for reading and learning, explains the instructional format of the book, and gives you an overview of each chapter. Chapter 2 defines the key concepts and explores the elements of the "production" of healthcare services. It also explains the key differences between healthcare processes and the individual "operations" or cycles of work that processes link together. Chapter 3 defines the key concept of a standard and explores the elements of a continuous improvement culture. Chapter 4 looks at standardization by discussing the importance of clear communication and guiding you through the stages of creating, maintaining, and improving standards. Chapter 5 focuses on standard work and discusses its important elements and formulas. In five steps—using five key tools—it explains how to achieve standard work. It also gives guidelines for how to maintain your standard operations. Chapter 6 furnishes several helpful examples of the applications of standardization and standard work in healthcare. A summary for implementing standard work is provided in Chapter 7. Finally, the Appendix provides numerous resources for learning more about standardization and standard work.

To be competitive in today's marketplace, you absolutely cannot afford to let rules and work processes be haphazard or become customary by default. You must give conscious, quality attention to applying standards, standardization, and standard work to your healthcare processes. *Standard Work for Lean Healthcare* shows you how.

Acknowledgments

The development of *Standard Work for Lean Healthcare* has been a team effort. Daksha Jackson of 6 Penang Street helped with the initial development of the draft. Heidi Butenschoen of Gehrschoen Creative helped with the artwork. Mike Rona, Patti Crome, Erin Ressler, and Dr. Sam Carlson of the Rona Consulting Group gave valuable feedback on the content of the book. I would also like to acknowledge the many talented people of the Productivity Press Development Team, and in particular Judith Allen, who created the original book, *Standard Work for the Shopfloor*, upon which much of this book is based.

We are very pleased to bring you this addition to our Lean Tools for Healthcare Series and wish you continued and increasing success on your Lean journey.

Thomas L. Jackson, Series Editor

Chapter 1

Getting Started

1.1 THE PURPOSE OF THIS BOOK

Key Point

Standard Work for Lean Healthcare was written to give you the information you need to implement standardization and standard work in your workplace. You are a valued member of your healthcare organization's transformation team; your knowledge, support, and participation are essential to the success of any major improvement effort in your organization.

You may be reading this book because your team leader or manager asked you to do so. Or you may be reading it because you think it will provide information that will help you in your work. By the time you finish Chapter 1, you will have a better idea of how the information in this book can help you and your organization eliminate waste and serve your patients more effectively.

1.2 WHAT THIS BOOK IS BASED ON

BACKGROUND INFO

This book is about an approach to implementing standardization and standard work methods designed to eliminate waste from healthcare processes. The methods and goals discussed here are closely related to the Lean production system developed at Toyota Motor Company. Since 1979, Productivity Press has brought knowledge and information about these approaches to the United States through publications, events, training, and consulting. Since 2007, the Rona Consulting Group has been applying this knowledge on the shop floor of healthcare. Today, top organizations around the world are applying Lean healthcare principles to improve patient safety and make healthcare more affordable. *Standard Work for Lean Healthcare* draws on a wide variety of Productivity's resources. Its aim is to present the main concepts and steps of implementing standards in a simple, illustrated format that is easy to read and understand.

1.3 TWO WAYS TO USE THIS BOOK

There are at least two ways to use this book:

1. As the reading material for a learning group or study group process within your organization.
2. For learning on your own.

Your organization may decide to design its own learning group process based on *Standard Work for Lean Healthcare.* Alternatively, you may read this book for individual learning without formal group discussion. Either way, you will learn valuable concepts and techniques to apply to your daily work.

1.4 HOW TO GET THE MOST OUT OF YOUR READING

1.4.1 Becoming Familiar with This Book

There are a few steps you can follow to make it easier to absorb the information in this book. Take as much time as you need to become familiar with the material. First, get a "big picture" view of the book by doing the following:

How-to Steps

- Scan the Table of Contents to see how *Standard Work for Lean Healthcare* is arranged.
- Read the rest of this introductory section for an overview of the book's contents.
- Flip through the book to get a feel for its style, flow, and design. Notice how the chapters are structured and glance at the illustrations.

1.4.2 Becoming Familiar with Each Chapter

After you have a sense of the overall structure of *Standard Work for Lean Healthcare,* prepare yourself to study one chapter at a time. For each chapter, we suggest you follow these steps to get the most out of your reading:

How-to Steps

- Flip through the chapter, looking at the way it is laid out. Notice the bold headings and the key points flagged in the margins.
- Now, read the chapter. How long this takes depends on what you already know about the content and what you are trying to get out of your reading. Enhance your reading by doing the following:
  - Use the margin assists to help you follow the flow of information.
  - If the book is your own, use a highlighter to mark key information and answers to your questions about the material. If the book is not your own, take notes on a separate piece of paper.
  - Answer the Take Five questions in the text. These will help you absorb the information by reflecting on how you might apply it to your own workplace.
- Read the Summary at the end of the chapter to reinforce what you have learned. If you read something in the summary that you do not remember, find that section in the chapter and review it.
- Finally, read the Reflections questions at the end of the chapter. Think about these questions and write down your answers.

1.4.3 How a Reading Strategy Works

When reading a book, many people think they should start with the first word and read straight through until the end. This is not usually the best way to learn from a book. The steps that were just presented for how to read this book are a strategy for making your reading easier, more fun, and more effective.

Reading strategy is based on two simple points about the way people learn. The first point is this: *It is difficult for your brain to absorb new information if it does not have a structure in which to place it.* As an analogy, imagine trying to build a house without first putting up a framework.

Like building a frame for a house, you can give your brain a framework for the new information in the book by getting an overview of the contents and then flipping through the materials. Within each chapter, you repeat this process on a smaller scale by reading the overview, key points, and headings before reading the text.

The second point about learning is this: *It is a lot easier to learn if you take in the information one layer at a time, instead of trying to absorb it all at once.* It is like finishing the walls of a house: First, you lay down a coat of primer. When that is dry, you apply a coat of paint, and later a final finish coat.

1.4.4 Using the Margin Assists

As you have noticed by now, this book uses small images called *margin assists* to help you follow the information in each chapter. There are eight types of margin assists:

INFO BACKGROUND	Background Information	Sets the stage for what comes next
VIEW OVER	Overview	Presents new information without the detail presented later
Definition	Definition	Explains how the author uses key terms
Key Point	Key Point	Highlights important ideas to remember
New Tool	New Tool	Helps you apply what you have learned

Example   Helps you understand the key points

 How-to Steps   Gives you a set of directions for using
                                     new instruments

 Principles   Explains how things work in a variety of
                                     situations

1.5 AN OVERVIEW OF THE CONTENTS

1.5.1 Chapter 1: Getting Started

Chapter 1, which you have been reading, has already explained the purpose of *Standard Work for Lean Healthcare* and how it was written. Then it shared tips for getting the most out of your reading. Now, it will present a brief description of each chapter.

1.5.2 Chapter 2: The Production of Healthcare Services

Chapter 2 describes the industrial origins of the Lean healthcare methodology and describes the critical distinction between healthcare processes and operations.

1.5.3 Chapter 3: Standards and Beyond

Chapter 3 defines the key terms—standard, standardization, and standard work. It explores the elements of a continuous improvement culture and describes standard work as the culmination of Lean healthcare implementation.

1.5.4 Chapter 4: Standardization

Chapter 4 describes standardization in more detail, discusses the importance of clear presentation of information about standards, and how to adhere to those standards, and walks through the critical steps of creating, maintaining, and improving standards.

1.5.5 Chapter 5: Standard Work

Chapter 5 defines standard work and describes the key formulas for calculating takt time, determining work sequence, standard work-in-process, and work area staffing through line balancing. It then details a four-step process of establishing standard operations, and describes how to use the various tables and work sheets to create standard operations.

1.5.6 Chapter 6: Applications of Standardization and Standard Work

Chapter 6 provides several examples of the applications of standardization and standard work. Applications to employee training, design, making improvements, healthcare management, and decision-making are discussed.

1.5.7 Chapter 7: Reflections and Conclusions

Chapter 7 presents reflections on and conclusions to this book. It includes a summary of the steps for standard work implementation. It also describes opportunities for further learning about techniques related to standardization and standard work.

Chapter 2

The Production Processes and Operations of Healthcare

2.1 THE INDUSTRIAL ORIGINS OF LEAN HEALTHCARE

The purpose of the *Lean Tools for Healthcare* Series is to introduce readers to a set of methods that have been proven to dramatically increase patient safety and reduce the cost of providing healthcare services. The term "Lean" was coined to express the notion that, like an athlete, an organization should be without organizational "fat" or what Lean specialists refer to as non-value-adding waste, where value refers to what a patient would be willing to pay for. Figure 2.1 lists seven distinct types of waste found in healthcare.

Lean tools and methods have important origins in the United States but were perfected principally within the Toyota Motor Company between 1948 and 1963, and have since been copied by most sectors of the manufacturing industry. The first major implementation in the healthcare industry began in 2001, when the Virginia Mason Medical Center in Seattle, Washington, engaged consultants (most of whom had been production engineers from Toyota and the Boeing Aircraft Company) to teach them how to apply the Toyota Production System to the production of healthcare services. A few years later, Park Nicollet Health Services in Minneapolis, Minnesota and

Seven Wastes in Healthcare Operations and Administration

Definitions	Healthcare Wastes	Administrative Wastes
1. Overproduction Producing more, sooner, or faster than is required by the next process	Performing services that patients do not need or desire. Unnecessary backups between departments. Multiple quality control checks.	Printing or processing reports, emails, or other information products before they are needed. Overdissemination of reports, etc.
2. Waiting Time delays, process idle time	Waiting for lab results. Waiting for doctors. Waiting for nurses. Waiting for decisions from hospital administrators. Idle people.	Searching for information. Waiting for information system response. Waiting for approvals from superiors.
3. Transportation Unnecessary handling or transportation; multiple handling	Excessive medical record pickups and deliveries. Extra handoffs. Excess patient transfer/movement.	Transferring data files between incompatible computer systems or software packages. Overdissemination of reports, etc.
4. Overprocessing Unnecessary processing, steps, or work elements/procedures	Asking the patient the same question 20 times. Multiple signatures. Extra copies of same form. Duplicate data input entries.	Re-entering data, extra copies; reformatting or excessive/custom formatting. Unnecessary reviews. Ccs on emails.
5. Inventory Producing, holding, or purchasing unnecessary inventory	Cabinets full of gloves. Piles of paper forms. Too many suture materials. Too many prosthetic devices. Multiple storage sites.	Decisions in process. Outdated, obsolete information in file cabinets or stored in databases.
6. Motion Excessive handling, unnecessary steps, non-ergonomic motion	Long reach/walk distances. Lifting more than 35 pounds, etc. Standing all day. Sitting all day. Not enough printers. Not enough copiers.	Repetitive stress injuries resulting from poor keyboard design. Excessive walking to and from remote printers.
7. Defects Rework, correction of errors, quality problems, equipment problems	Adverse events. High infection rates. Wrong meds. Wrong surgical site. Frequent rescheduling. Patient readmissions.	Order-entry errors. Too many bill rejects. Design errors and engineering change orders. Invoice errors. Info system downtime.

FIGURE 2.1 The seven wastes. (Reprinted with permission. J. Michael Rona and Associates, LLC, doing business as Rona Consulting Group © 2008–2011 ©. All rights reserved. http://www.ronaconsulting.com.)

a few other organizations, including Thedacare in Wisconsin launched another major implementation. The success of these implementations is well documented.*

Naturally, readers coming to the subject of Lean healthcare for the first time are often perplexed by the patently industrial point of view taken by Lean healthcare specialists. How can healthcare be treated as an industrial process? Isn't medicine an art? Can healthcare processes be standardized when all patients are unique? In fact, medicine and healthcare practice are generally becoming more scientific or evidence-based, and the Center for Medicare & Medicaid Services (CMS) and deeming authorities such as The Joint Commission are quick to require adherence to standardized, evidence-based practices. Moreover, industrial engineering has long been applied to healthcare processes. Some readers may recall actor Clifton Web's portrayal of the time-and-motion consultant Frank Gilbreth in the 1950 movie *Cheaper by the Dozen*. The movie depicts Gilbreth's groundbreaking time and motion studies of surgery in hospital operating rooms. In many ways, the practice of Lean healthcare continues in the tradition of Gilbreth's time studies. The major difference, as we will see in Chapter 5, is that the studies are not carried out by consultants; the studies are conducted by members of the healthcare team (clinicians and support staff), frequently with the voluntary participation of patients themselves.

2.2 PRODUCTION, PROCESS, AND OPERATION

Before studying Lean healthcare, you must understand precisely how the notion of "production" applies to the production of healthcare services.† As perplexing as it may seem, production is not necessarily an activity that requires machines.

---

* John Black with David Miller, *The Toyota Way to Healthcare Excellence: Increase Efficiency and Improve Quality with Lean* (Chicago: Health Administration Press, 2008).

† Much of this chapter paraphrases, in language friendly to healthcare, Chapter 1 of Shigeo Shingo's groundbreaking book, *A Study of the Toyota Production System from an Industrial Engineering Perspective* (Cambridge, MA: Productivity Press, 1989).

Definition

Production is the making of either a product or a service—it does not matter which.

Obviously, artisans produced goods and services before the advent of steam power. In its most general sense, production is simply a network of what industrial engineers call processes and operations.

Definition

A *process* is a sequence of cycles of work called "operations." An *operation* is a work cycle defined by a sequence of specific tasks.

Figure 2.2 illustrates how a healthcare process—transforming a patient from the state of "unhealthy" to "healthy"—is accomplished through a series of medical and other healthcare operations. When we look at a healthcare process over time (especially when we see it from the patient's perspective), we see flows of patients, clinicians, medicines, supplies, and equipment in time and space. We see the transformation

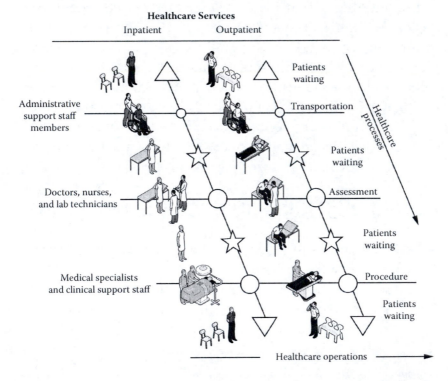

FIGURE 2.2 The healthcare service production process. (Reprinted with permission. J. Michael Rona and Associates, LLC, doing business as Rona Consulting Group, and iStockphoto LP © 2008–2011 ©. All rights reserved. http://www.ronaconsulting.com; http://istockphoto.com)

of the patient from the moment at which she presents undiagnosed symptoms, to initial assessment, definitive diagnosis, and finally to treatment and recovery. When we look at operations, on the other hand, we see the work performed by doctors, nurses, lab technicians, pharmacists, etc. to accomplish this transformation—the interaction of patients, clinicians, medicines, and healthcare equipment in time and space.

To make fundamental improvement in the process of producing healthcare services, we must distinguish between the flow of patients (process) from the clinical work flow (operation) and analyze them separately. This is why in Figure 2.2 we have illustrated healthcare production as a network of process and operation. The analysis of healthcare processes examines the flow of patients; the analysis of healthcare operations examines the work performed on patients by clinicians and support staff, medicines, and healthcare equipment. Consider a typical patient, a patient who makes a visit to an outpatient clinic. The patient is registered at the front desk and then asked to wait. Then a nurse calls the patient and escorts her to an examination room. The nurse may take the patient's blood pressure and ask questions to make an initial assessment of the patient's condition. Next, the doctor interviews the patient and reaches a diagnosis. After this, the patient receives some treatment, let us say an injection administered by a nurse, who first draws the prescribed medication and after sterilizing the patient's arm injects the medication into the patient's bloodstream. This series of changes in the patient (from undiagnosed to treated) is process. The nurse's actions of filling the syringe, sterilizing the patient's arm, and injecting the medication into the patient constitute an operation.

2.3 SUMMARY

All production, whether carried out in any healthcare setting—in the operating room, the clinic, the lab, or the pharmacy—must be understood as a functional network of process and operation. Healthcare processes transform unwell patients into well patients. Healthcare operations are the clinical actions that accomplish those transformations. These fundamental concepts and their relationship must be understood in order to make effective, evidence-based improvements in the production of healthcare services.

REFLECTIONS

Now that you have completed this chapter, take five minutes to think about these questions and write down your answers.

1. What did you learn from reading this chapter that stands out as being particularly useful or interesting to you in healthcare?
2. How do you feel about the idea of "producing" healthcare services using industrial methods?
3. Do you have any questions about the topics presented in this chapter? If so, what are they?
4. Are there any special obstacles in your mind or the minds of your colleagues to applying the distinction between process and operation in healthcare?
5. What information do you still need to understand fully the ideas presented?
6. How can you get this information?
7. Whom do you need to involve in this process?

Chapter 3

Standards and Beyond

3.1 WHAT IS A STANDARD?

Definition

In healthcare we spend too much time arguing about what standard to follow (e.g., how to wean a patient from a ventilator) because there are many times when "expert opinion" rules, and everyone is an expert. It is far more important first to agree to a standard practice, follow it, and then improve it. This is critical to the idea of a healthcare standard, such as stepped diabetes care or hardwiring the practice of immunization or adherence to CMS core measures. A standard is a rule or example that provides clear expectations. Continuous improvement methods depend on identifying, setting, and improving standards. Without an initial standard, how can you measure the effectiveness of the improvements you make to achieve that standard? How can you improve the standard? How can you set additional goals and know if you have achieved them? Standards form the *baseline* for all improvement activities, and new standards define the *breakthrough goals* you strive to achieve as your continuous improvement activities gain momentum.

3.1.1 Characteristics of Standards

Key Point

Standards must be specific and scientific—meaning that they are based on facts (or *evidence*) and analysis, not on custom, guessing, or memory.

Key Point

Standards must be adhered to. They are useless if no one follows them. For a standard to *be* a standard, it will be *consistently followed and respected*.

Example

An example of a standard in the context of traffic regulation is a red light at an intersection. What makes this

Example

a standard is that people actually stop when the light turns red. Accidents occur when the standard is not followed.

Another example is a four-way stop sign. When two cars come to an intersection at once, the person on the right has the right-of-way. If the two drivers do not know this rule, then they may sit there for a long time wondering what to do, or both may go at once and cause an accident.

Key Point

Standards must be documented and communicated so that people will know what they are and will be able to follow them.

3.1.2 Sources and Types of Standards

There are three sources of standards:

1. Those based on authority or custom that evolve slowly over time.
2. Those based on scientific data, evidence, or experience that evolve continually, but more quickly than standards based on authority and custom.
3. Those based on technical specifications that tend to remain constant.

3.1.3 Standards and Standard Work versus Best Practice

It is important to distinguish between standards, standard work, and best practice. A best practice is a healthcare practice that stands as a recognized benchmark in the industry, but which has been implemented by someone else. Standards and standard work are the means by which we systematically test and—if appropriate—adopt a best practice in our own facility, frequently with important changes geared to the personnel, facilities, and work culture of our own organization. In addition, unlike a "best practice," standards are designed to be tested and changed because there will always be opportunities for improvement no matter how "good" the "best practice" may be. The implementation of standard work is never a one-for-one adoption of another facility's best practice. Otherwise, we run the risk of benchmarking mediocrity.

TAKE FIVE

Take five minutes to think about these questions and write down your answers:

1. What are some standards based on *custom* in your workplace?
2. Which ones do you think need improvement?

3.2 WHAT IS STANDARDIZATION?

Definition

Standardization is the practice of setting, communicating, following, and improving standards. Today healthcare may still be more of an art than a science, but the trend toward evidence-based practice based upon disciplined, scientific inquiry is clear. More and more, reliable medical practice and healthcare processes depend on standardization. Standardization facilitates measurement—the gathering of data and information—and promotes consistency in application through uniform criteria and practices. First you observe your process, then you improve it, then you standardize it. You *define the process* so that everyone can see it and know what it is—and can follow it. For example, in the 5S activity for improving workplace organization, the fourth S is "standardize"—make rules for maintaining the improvements achieved in the first three Ss.*

In continuous improvement, you measure the effects of your improvements in relation to the initial standard and its associated results. If you get better results with the improved process, then the standard can be changed. If the results are not better, the original standard should remain unchanged. In this way, standards require you to prove with facts, with evidence, that the changes you make actually improve the

---

* See *5S for Healthcare* (New York: Productivity Press, 2009).

process. Without the standard to measure against, there would be no improvement process you could depend on, and no way to know how to improve it or know whether you had improved it.

Key Point

This process of continually improving the standards is the path to reliable methods—the effective and efficient sequence of operations that is a key component of standard work.

Key Point

Everyone must practice the standards consistently before standardization truly exists. Consequently, standardization depends on user-friendly language, pictures, or symbols to communicate the standard. It must be easy to see and understand what the standard is so that everyone can learn to practice it. *When 100 percent adherence to reliable methods occurs, you have standardization.* For example, everyone knows how important hand washing is to infection control, and it is certainly the policy of every hospital that staff members should wash their hands. However, when staff members wash their hands only 30 percent of the time, the policy fails to become a standard.

In Figure 3.1, you can see that there are a number of levels to achieving standardization throughout an organization for

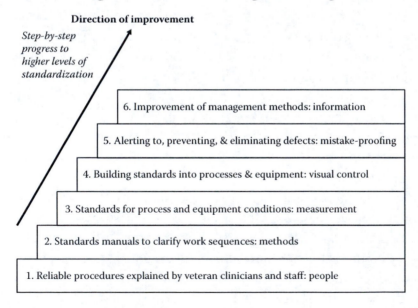

FIGURE 3.1 The implementation ladder of standardization. (Reproduced from *Standard Work for the Shopfloor*, p. 5, Productivity Press, New York, 2002. With permission.)

its full benefits to be felt. Most manufacturing organizations have achieved level 2—the second rung of the ladder of standardization. Lean manufacturing organizations, those that have adopted the Toyota Management System, have reached higher levels. When Lean operations are implemented and standardization of these reliable methods is achieved, standards are built into the operations themselves as shown in the third, fourth, and fifth rungs of the ladder. Standardized management methods are the final rung of the standardization ladder.* Although there are a few Lean healthcare organizations, most healthcare organizations are at level 1 and have a long way to go.

TAKE FIVE

Take five minutes to think about these questions and write down your answers:

1. Does everyone follow the standards set for your operations line? Do you?
2. Can you identify one standard that needs greater adherence to be effective?

Aspects of standardization are described in detail in Chapter 5.

3.3 WHAT IS STANDARD WORK?

Definition

Standard work is an agreed-upon set of work procedures that establish the best and most reliable methods and sequences for each clinician and support staff member. It is also a method that helps determine those methods and sequences. Standard work aims to maximize performance while minimizing waste in *each person's* operation and workload.

Key Point

Medicine is both an art and a science; therefore, it is important to be very clear—standard work is not a rigid "work

---

* For examples of what standardized management methods look like, see, for example, *Hoshin Kanri for the Lean Enterprise* (Portland, OR: Productivity Press, 2006).

standard" that never changes. Rather, *standard work is the fluctuating level of optimum work to be done by clinicians and staff members each day to meet patient demand.* As you will learn by reading this book, it is determined precisely, through a series of calculations, so that the rate of patient demand, known as "takt time," can be adhered to by each clinician and staff member and every service line, department, or work area. Optimum workflow, physical layouts, and work in process and inventory levels are all considered in the standard work method.

3.3.1 Lean Healthcare Methods = Standard Processes and Reliable Methods

Key Point

Standard work is a tool used in healthcare to best utilize people at their various levels of licensure while keeping the rhythm of operations tied to the flow of patient requirements.

We have discussed standards, standardization, and reliable methods as the basis of continuous improvement. The methods that comprise Lean healthcare (5S, quick setup, mistake-proofing, etc.) are themselves considered to be the reliable methods of operations. You may find ways to improve or adjust these methods for your own workplace, but these already have been proven reliable in a wide variety of contexts, including healthcare. This means that wherever they are applied, in whatever industry or culture, and for whatever service being made, these methods work—they are methods designed to create services with the highest patient safety, with the highest quality, in the shortest time, and at the lowest cost. They ensure safety and support human autonomy and creativity. They deliver to the patient what she needs, when she needs it, and in the required quantity. Standard work is driven by improvement; it is not a rigid, unchanging rule but *a flexible response to current conditions in the workplace and in the market.*

3.3.2 Standard Work Is a Prerequisite of Lean Healthcare

Standard work is the prerequisite to the implementation of all the other instruments in the methodology of Lean healthcare, including:

- 5S and visual control
- Continuous flow
- Mistake-proofing and autonomation (*jidoka*)
- Quick setup
- Kanban and pull operations
- Management by means (*hoshin kanri*)
- Standardized problem solving

What makes Lean healthcare unique is the systematic application of the scientific method by all clinicians, support staff, and administrators—no matter their level of licensure or managerial responsibility. Each of the Lean methods listed previously requires the application of the scientific method by individuals directly involved in the processes of healthcare delivery or administration. Standard work is in fact a foundational element of all Lean healthcare practice. Not only does it reduce manageable variation in all processes, it also creates a framework for the systematic measurement—and therefore improvement—of performance.

3.3.3 Standard Work Drives Further Improvement

Key Point

Standard work functions as a diagnostic tool, exposing problems and inspiring continual improvement. It supports process standardization and further elimination of waste throughout the operations process. With standard work in place, every doctor, nurse, lab technician, and pharmacist becomes a scientist, continually finding waste and experimenting to remove it from the workplace.

Chapters 4 and 5 describe the standard work calculations and documentation in detail.

TAKE FIVE

Take five minutes to think about these questions and write down your answers:

1. What is a reliable method?
2. What makes Lean healthcare operations a set of reliable methods?
3. What are some characteristics of standard work?

3.4 STANDARD WORK AND EVIDENCE-BASED PRACTICE

In this chapter, we have mentioned numerous characteristics of standardization and standard work. These characteristics can be summarized as being:

- An agreed-upon best way to perform each operation and process—the documented standards and standard work procedures.
- The discipline to adhere to the standards—standardization.
- A framework for gathering accurate data by measuring performance in terms of deviations from established standards to which clinicians and support staff routinely adhere.
- A mechanism for improving documented, reliable methods—formal evidence gathering, idea generation, and continuous improvement methods.

3.4.1 Evidence-Based Practice

As stated before, healthcare is both an art and a science. A deep understanding of the methodologies and conclusions of evidence is the science, and the understanding of the nuances that lead to applying the science successfully to the individual patient is the art. You must have both. It is true that patients

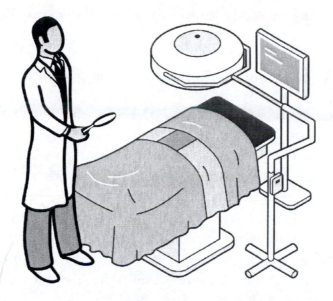

FIGURE 3.2 Standard work makes everyone a scientist. (Reprinted with permission. J. Michael Rona and Associates, LLC, doing business as Rona Consulting Group, and iStockphoto LP © 2008–2011 ©. All rights reserved. http://www.ronaconsulting.com; http://istock photo.com.)

present unique symptoms in unique ways that will always engage the creative faculties of physicians and medical scientists. It is also true that there is a growing body of evidence that strongly suggests that much if not most of healthcare practices can and should be standardized to improve patient safety and the quality of clinical outcomes. Moreover, it is clear that the CMS and deeming agencies such as The Joint Commission have taken a forceful position in ensuring that evidence-based practices be adopted.

Key Point

In this context, standardization and standard work may be understood as two very powerful tools with which to translate the benchmarks—or academic knowledge—of evidence-based practice into action. While evidence-based practice tells us what has worked elsewhere, standardization and standard work give us a concrete methodology that helps prepare for implementation by first observing what it is we ourselves are doing. In addition, they give us a way to imbed the new practice into our own operations and processes by carefully training our clinicians and support staff and again helping them adhere to the new practice.

3.4.2 A Culture of Continuous Improvement

A culture of standard work and continuous improvement should already be in place if you are implementing lean operations (i.e., evidence-based healthcare) in your hospitals, clinics, labs, and pharmacies. This means that there are formal methods practiced by everyone for improving operations: weekly team activities, documented process analysis, and mechanisms for gathering data, reporting findings, and gaining approval for making changes in the current methods. Figure 3.3 shows that there are many control points for improving standards throughout the operations process.

Clinicians and support staff in Lean healthcare organizations are continually thinking of ways to improve the way

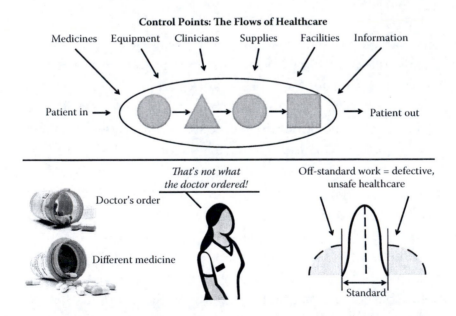

FIGURE 3.3 Elements for building quality and safety into healthcare operations. (Reprinted with permission. J. Michael Rona and Associates, LLC, doing business as Rona Consulting Group, and iStockphoto LP. ©2008–2011©. All rights reserved. http://www.rona consulting.com; http://istockphoto.com)

they do their work. The culture must support this creative problem solving if standardization is to be achieved and the flexibility of standard work is to be possible. What can you do to support continuous improvement within the context of standardized and standard work environments?

- Support teamwork and ownership of the process by every clinician and staff member.
- Reward clinicians and support staff who suggest improvements.
- Allow (do not punish) mistakes and encourage experimentation (within the framework of standard work).
- Create a system for capturing and implementing employee suggestions.
- Provide collaboration with specialists to support team improvement activities.
- Train every clinician and staff member when new standard work is introduced.
- Offer training to every clinician and staff member on improvement methods.

It is important to recognize a critical and perhaps unexpected characteristic of creating standards, standardization, and standard work: they are not only the *result* of initial improvement activities, they also *drive continual improvement*. However, the improvements made must be based on evidence gathered from the baseline of the standard that has been described, agreed upon, and adhered to by all.

Key Point

Only when you have standardization can you systematically improve healthcare operations without creating chaos, and thereby gain adherence throughout the system when a better way is discovered. Standard work itself is intended to create a flexible and responsive workplace, where clinicians and support staff can move to the operations most needed to meet patient demand. Without standardization—adherence to the set standards—this orderly flexibility and responsiveness will be impossible to achieve.

TAKE FIVE

Take five minutes to think about these questions and write down your answers:

1. What is needed for a culture of continuous improvement to exist in healthcare?
2. Which of these is in place in your workplace?

3.5 THE BENEFITS OF STANDARDIZATION AND STANDARD WORK

3.5.1 For the Organization

Standardization and standard work benefit your organization by enabling:

- Reduced variability, reduced waste, and reduced costs
- Improved quality and shorter, more predictable lead times
- The achievement of certification by your chosen deeming authority, that is, The Joint Commission or the International Standards Organization (ISO)

3.5.2 For Patients

Standardization and standard work benefit patients through:

- Improved access to needed healthcare services
- Improved patient safety
- Reduced cost

3.5.3 For Clinicians and Support Staff

Standardization and standard work benefit clinicians and support staff by making it:

- Easier to learn new protocols and processes
- Easier to see problems and contribute improvement ideas

SUMMARY

A standard is a rule or example that provides clear expectations. Continuous improvement methods depend on identifying, setting, and improving standards. Standards form the baseline for all improvement activities, and they define the breakthrough goals you strive to achieve as your continuous improvement activities gain momentum. Standards must be specific and scientific—meaning that they are based on facts and analysis, not on custom, guessing, or memory. Standards must be adhered to; they are useless if no one follows them. For a standard to be a standard, it will be followed consistently and respected. In addition, standards must be documented and communicated so that people will know what they are and will be able to follow them.

Standardization is the practice of setting, communicating, following, and improving standards. Healthcare processes depend on standardization. Standardization promotes consistency through uniform criteria and practices. In 5S, the fourth S is "standardize"—make the rules for maintaining the improvements achieved in the first three Ss. First you improve your process, then you standardize it. You define the process so that everyone knows what it is and can follow it. Everyone must practice the standards consistently before standardization truly exists.

Standard work is an agreed-upon set of work procedures that establish the best and most reliable methods and sequences for each process and each clinician. It is also a method that helps determine those methods and sequences. Standard work aims to maximize performance while minimizing waste in each person's operation and workload. Standard work is not a best practices or rigid "work standard" that never changes; rather, standard work is the fluctuating level of optimum work to be done by clinicians and support staff each day to meet patient demand. It is determined precisely, through a series of calculations, so that takt time can be adhered to by each operator and every department or work area. Optimum work in process and inventory levels, cycle time, and physical layouts of facilities are all considered in the standard work method. Standard work is a tool used in cellular healthcare and pull operations to best utilize doctors, nurses, lab technicians, and pharmacists while keeping the rhythm of operations tied to the flow of patient orders. It is a flexible response to current conditions in the workplace and in the marketplace.

It is important to recognize a critical and perhaps unexpected characteristic of creating standards, standardization, and standard work: they are not only the result of initial improvement activities; they also drive continual improvement. Only when you have standardization can you systematically improve your operations without creating chaos, and thereby gain adherence throughout the system when a better way is discovered. Standard work itself is intended to provide a flexible and responsive workplace, where clinicians and support staff can move to the operations most needed to meet patient demand. Without standardization—adherence to set standards—this orderly flexibility and responsiveness will be impossible to achieve.

Standardization and standard work benefit your organization by reducing variability, waste, and costs. They help improve quality and shorten lead times, and they lead the way to certification by healthcare deeming authorities such as The Joint Commission or ISO. Standardization and standard work benefit you by making it easier for you to learn new operations, and easier for you to shift to different operations within a cell or move to other cells, lines, or work areas. They also provide the baseline for contributing new improvement ideas.

REFLECTIONS

Now that you have completed this chapter, take five minutes to think about these questions and write down your answers:

1. What did you learn from reading this chapter that stands out as particularly useful or interesting?

2. Do you have any questions about the topics presented in this chapter? If so, what are they?
3. What additional information do you need to understand fully the ideas presented in this chapter?

Chapter 4

Standardization

In Chapter 3, we defined standardization as including the following three aspects:

1. The path to reliable methods
2. 100 percent adherence to reliable methods (through good communication)
3. Creating and maintaining improvements to standards

These all relate to the process of creating safe, high-quality healthcare services at the lowest cost and in the shortest time. Chapter 4 discusses these three elements of standardization in further detail.

4.1 THE PATH TO RELIABLE METHODS

Figure 4.1 displays a formula for establishing standards that combines the process standards and technical standards. In other words, standardization must incorporate both the service and the process standards to be effective in assuring the lowest cost, highest quality, and shortest delivery time for each healthcare service.

4.1.1 Types of In-House Standards

Figure 4.2 shows a list of nine types of in-house standards and the documents used in most healthcare organizations to communicate them.

Key Point

4.1.2 100 Percent Adherence to Reliable Methods

Whether standards define a medical protocol or a healthcare process such as a treatment plan, standardization

| Technical standards | × | Process standards | = | Standards |

Establishes medical, nursing, pharmaceutical and laboratory protocols for preparing and administering healthcare treatments.

Describes techniques for regulating healthcare's many handoffs and to coordinate protocols of care and use equipment, medicines, and supplies to make the work flow of healthcare more reliable, less expensive, more timely, and safer for the patient, clinicians, and staff.

FIGURE 4.1 Formula for establishing standards. (Reproduced from *Standard Work for the Shopfloor*, p. 14, Productivity Press, New York, 2002. With permission.)

Type	Description
1. Regulations	These are formally established task and process management methods imposed by regulatory agencies such as the Center for Medicare & Medicaid Services (CMS) and deeming authorities such as The Joint Commission, as well as other federal, state, and local regulatory agencies.
2. Quality policies	These are service quality regulations based upon service standards specified by patients and other customers of organization and adopted as in-house standards for services and inspection procedures.
3. Specifications	These are restrictions and other conditions placed on suppliers of medicines, supplies, equipment, and tools and agreed on during supply contract negotiations.
4. Healthcare policies	These are the detailed standards concerning the performance of medical, nursing, laboratory, pharmaceutical, or other healthcare-related procedures. They stipulate how these procedures are to be performed by licensed professionals.
5. Other technical standards	These are the detailed standards concerning the many other dimensions of healthcare processes such as food services, environmental services, etc.
6. Process standards	These describe work procedures (processes). They usually appear in work procedure sheets or work instruction booklets.
7. Manuals	These are handbooks used for training and for detailed descriptions of work methods. They also define the organization's standards and objectives.
8. Circular notices	These notices inform people of new or revised standards, necessary preparations or response, and other related matters.
9. Memos	Memos are a common means of communication for prior notification of extraordinary measures, temporary revisions, or other standard-related matters. They are also for other types of notices, such as meeting minutes or in-house reports.

FIGURE 4.2 Types and purposes of in-house policies and standards for healthcare. (Reproduced from *Standard Work for the Shopfloor*, p. 15, Productivity Press, New York, 2002. With permission.)

depends on communication of the standard for 100 percent adherence to be achieved. Adherence to standards is the key to a strong improvement culture. *It is critical that you communicate the standards simply and easily so that everyone knows what they are and can follow them.*

4.2 COMMUNICATING IN-HOUSE POLICIES AND STANDARDS

Every healthcare organization has its policies, which are a type of in-house standard, that define the way that things should be done. Good policy manuals are hard to come by. Often, the information in manuals is obscure or hard to find.

Policy manuals should include descriptions that are easy to understand, in language that conforms to the standards and conventions of each hospital. All departments that need to refer to the same manuals should be able to understand them equally well. If different departments use different terms for the same things, all relevant terms should be included and defined. Standard formats should be adaptable so that only slight revisions to the manuals are required when medical protocols or healthcare processes change. Information in manuals should be clearly oriented to its primary objective: maintaining high service quality and clinical performance.

Policy manuals should include only those items that must be adhered to by everyone. Those things that may be *preferred* by some do not belong in the manual. A good exercise for a clinic or hospital would be to identify those items that must be adhered to and those that are optional, and then separate them. Do it twice. Think carefully about what must be done and narrow this list down to the minimum items that cannot be ignored. This will help your clinicians and support staff enormously to simplify the process of learning and checking while healthcare is underway.

You can save time in updating changes if policies are kept in computer files. They can be easily accessed by anyone if they are stored as shared files. Items that do not need to be checked frequently can be moved to separate policy sheets or manuals. Items that need to be checked often should be positioned in each work area in clear, easy-to-read formats, using as much visual information as possible.

TAKE FIVE

Take five minutes to think about these questions and write down your answers:

1. Where do you keep your policy manuals? When was the last time you referred to one of them?
2. What are three policies you frequently need to refer to in your work area to ensure that you are meeting the in-house requirements for that operation?
3. What is one way you could improve your access to this information?

4.2.1 Often Manuals Are Not Designed for the User

Standards manuals typically are difficult to read, and therefore difficult to follow. The organization of the material may not be clear or conform to the actual sequence that clinicians and support staff must follow. Therefore, information is difficult to find when it is needed. Checklisted items abound in manuals, but often their significance is unclear or unstated. They may not be prioritized by importance or level of information, making it easy to overlook the most critical items. Standard procedure manuals may contain terms that are either too technical or too simplistic to be useful to the clinician or support staff member who needs the information to complete a process. Finally, manuals generally fail to describe how new hires can become veterans, making the information useless in building 100 percent adherence to the standards, the primary purpose of standardization itself.

4.2.2 Revisions Are Unsystematic

Manuals often remain unrevised for long periods even though the standards themselves have been changed and improved.

FIGURE 4.3 Poor communication of standards. (Reproduced from *Standard Work for the Shopfloor*, p. 17, Productivity Press, New York, 2002. With permission.)

Automated systems and mistake-proofing devices may have replaced obsolete checking procedures and data reporting methods described in older manuals. This creates confusion if workers do turn to manuals for clarification. What most often happens is that out-of-date manuals, which workers learn to ignore, become no more than useless inventory using up space on computer drives and in work areas. Redundancy may exist between manuals and discrepancies may exist between associates' notebooks and the information or language in the manuals. There may be no system for reviewing, evaluating, and revising the manuals, or manuals may be changed so frequently that they become unwieldy and confusing. Either way, this unsystematic approach to documenting standard procedures only leads to confusion and lack of standardization on the shop floor of healthcare.

4.2.3 Manuals Are Not Designed to Be Improved

As Lean healthcare methods are established, inspection becomes part of every operation in every work area. Since most operation manuals include checking and inspection points, redundancy occurs unless the manuals are revised as the new methods become standardized. In addition, checkpoints are often added to the operating procedure to address uninvestigated causes of process difficulties. However, if continuous improvement activities are well established, this should not occur because (as we will discuss in Chapter 5) quality and safety checkpoints will be deeply imbedded in standard work.

Finally, standardization depends on procedures being fully described so that clinicians and support staff know what to do when problems arise. If process values are outside control levels, standard procedures must tell everyone how to correct the variances. If protocols or processes cause defects, clinicians or support staff must know how to, and have the autonomy to "stop the line" to fix the problem. Empowerment must exist for each clinician or support staff member to check and correct any defects that may be produced, and to return any defects received from upstream so that no defects move downstream. Clear directions about what to do when standards are not followed or variances from standards occur are also part of the standardization process and must be clearly and visually displayed so that everyone is adequately informed.

TAKE FIVE

Take five minutes to think about these questions and write down your answers:

1. What do you need to know to do your work well?
2. Whom do you need to ask?
3. When and where do you need to know it? On a computer? At your fingertips?
4. What do you need to do so you have information when and where you need it?

4.3 WHAT TO INCLUDE IN STANDARDS DOCUMENTATION

4.3.1 Technical and Process Standards Sheets

Standards should be only one page, if possible, so that clinicians or support staff who need to refer to them can quickly

FIGURE 4.4 Good communication standards. (Reproduced from *Standard Work for the Shopfloor*, p. 18, Productivity Press, New York, 2002. With permission.)

see what is required. Technical and process standards should ideally include the following features:

Example

1. Clear objectives of the standards
2. Control points, checkpoints, and other management data—in both sentence form and symbols
3. Checkpoints divided into categories of "must" and "prefer," indicating both normal and abnormal ranges of operation
4. Data charts that can be easily used during healthcare service operations, using photos and drawings to show complex information

Standards sheets should be posted at the work site. Color-code the displays. Train employees in new standards so that 100 percent adherence can be achieved.

4.3.2 Equipment Manuals

In this age of high technology, sophisticated equipment abounds in healthcare operations. But who knows what to do when a vital piece of equipment malfunctions or fails?

Equipment manuals should explain troubleshooting procedures, motion principles, and parts structures, as well as include parts service and supplier addresses. Equipment standards manuals should include the following features:

Example

1. Main title indicating the purpose of the manual
2. Statement of scope or intended range of use
3. Table of contents including titles of sections and subsections in each chapter
4. Flowchart describing the information covered in the manual
5. Section and subsection titles that name the central issues discussed in the text
6. Troubleshooting directions
7. Equipment maintenance points and parts replacement and service periods
8. Contact information of critical on-site equipment support staff
9. Addresses of suppliers

4.4 THE VALUE OF USER-FRIENDLY STANDARDS

When standards are communicated so that they are easy to find and use, many benefits result:

1. *Patients are not harmed.* Because quality and safety are built into each process, fewer defective services are produced.
2. *Overtime goes down* as employee skills and morale increase. The path from novice to veteran is easier and clearer and boosts enthusiasm, self-confidence, skill, and satisfaction.
3. *Medicines and supplies are not wasted* as clinicians and staff learn to rely upon standard work in process. The reliability of the supply chain eliminates the need for hoarding.
4. *Healthcare service delivery delays diminish.* Patients and staff alike no longer wait because process and

equipment failures decrease and healthcare operations become more reliable.

5. *Patient satisfaction increases.* Quality standards and delivery schedules are met consistently.

4.5 CREATING AND MAINTAINING IMPROVEMENTS TO STANDARDS

The creation of standards and establishing standardization are important steps in any systematic continuous improvement activity. You must set up a spiral of improvement in standard operations that becomes an integral part of daily work. Figure 4.5 shows that the spiral is defined by the Deming cycle of Plan-Do-Check-Act (PDCA).

- Plan. First you must "go see" your current operations to truly understand what is going on, before you search for the root cause of problems and certainly before you brainstorm improvements. Solutions can then become part of the operating standard.

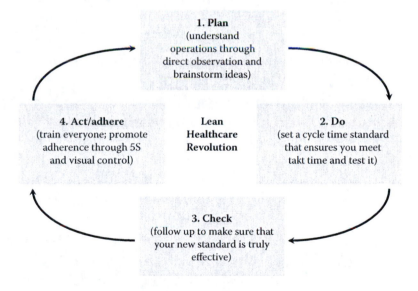

FIGURE 4.5 The spiral of improvement in standard operations. (Reproduced from *Standard Work for the Shopfloor*, p. 23, Productivity Press, New York, 2002. With permission.)

- Do. First, they must be tested to make sure that your new standards actually support your meeting patient requirements.
- Check. Next, you must follow up rigorously to see that the new standard is robust enough to withstand the pressures of actual work.
- Act. Finally, you must train everyone in the new standard and promote adherence with the Lean tools of 5S (workplace organization) and visual control.

TAKE FIVE

Take five minutes to think about these questions and write down your answers:

1. Can you identify a problem in your work where more training will help resolve the issue?
2. Are there any problems in your work area that you have been avoiding by adding steps to your operation? Are these added steps documented? Have you discussed them with your improvement team?
3. Have you gone to the actual work area to see the work being performed?
4. Have you tested new ideas before implementing them?

4.5.1 How Do You Create Standards and Standard Operations?

The improvement example just given and the spiral depicted in Figure 4.5 are versions of the familiar PDCA cycle in Total Quality Improvement. Standardization can easily be misunderstood if it is not recognized as just one recurring phase in this four-phase cycle.

Key Point

Standardization is not only adherence to standards but also the continual creation of new and better standards. Let us look more closely at this process to understand standardization more fully.

4.5.2 Stages of Standards Improvement

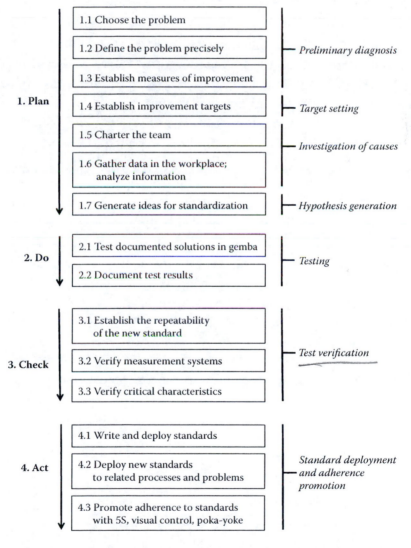

How-to Steps

In Figure 4.6, a complete PDCA sequence for solving problems is shown. This is the *process* of standardization. Let us examine it step by step.

Actually, we begin at the end, at Step 4.3, because improvement always begins with adherence to existing standards. The second step is 1.1, choosing the right problem to work

1. Plan	1.1 Choose the problem	
	1.2 Define the problem precisely	Preliminary diagnosis
	1.3 Establish measures of improvement	
	1.4 Establish improvement targets	Target setting
	1.5 Charter the team	Investigation of causes
	1.6 Gather data in the workplace; analyze information	
	1.7 Generate ideas for standardization	Hypothesis generation
2. Do	2.1 Test documented solutions in gemba	Testing
	2.2 Document test results	
3. Check	3.1 Establish the repeatability of the new standard	Test verification
	3.2 Verify measurement systems	
	3.3 Verify critical characteristics	
4. Act	4.1 Write and deploy standards	Standard deployment and adherence promotion
	4.2 Deploy new standards to related processes and problems	
	4.3 Promote adherence to standards with 5S, visual control, poka-yoke	

FIGURE 4.6 Standardization sequence for solving problems. (Reproduced from *Standard Work for the Shopfloor*, p. 25, Productivity Press, New York, 2002. With permission.)

on. Problems come from many places, but generally, they exist in two forms, as shown in Figure 4.7:

1. As variances from the established standard (Case 1)
2. As variances between actual conditions and the projected future standard—the improvement goal (Case 2)

Once we choose a problem to work on, we must define it precisely (Step 1.2) and establish measures of improvement (Step 1.3) so that we can know that we are getting better. How will you know when you have solved the problem? What measure will indicate this? Having established the measure of improvement, we establish specific improvement targets (Step 1.4) that ensure we will meet our patients' requirements. Next, we charter an improvement team (Step 1.5) that will gather information by making direct observations of the process (Step 1.6). We will see how to do this in Chapter 5 by conducting running time studies. You may also use a checklist (Figure 4.8) to find guidelines for discovering the root cause. A cause-and-effect diagram can be used to great advantage here. It is essential that you actually go to the work site and closely examine the operation or process being improved so that you do not make incorrect assumptions about the actual causes, which will cause you to solve the wrong problem, fail to find the *root cause,* and therefore have a return of the problem later or miss the real issues in some other way. You may want to ask

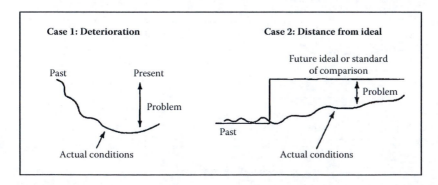

FIGURE 4.7 Two forms of problems and how they occur. (Reproduced from *Standard Work for the Shopfloor,* p. 26, Productivity Press, New York, 2002. With permission.)

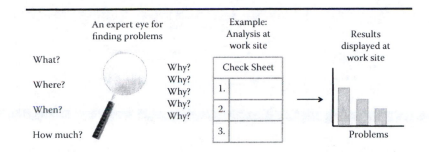

FIGURE 4.8 Checklist for finding the facts at the work site. (Reprinted with permission. J. Michael Rona and Associates, LLC, doing business as Rona Consulting Group, and iStockphoto LP. ©2008–2011©. All rights reserved. http://www.ronaconsulting.com; http://istockphoto.com)

an expert to help you identify what is going on to understand fully what you are addressing. The last step of the Plan phase of our improvement is to brainstorm ideas for improvement.

In the Do phase of the improvement process, we test documented solutions in the workplace (Step 2.1) and document test results (Step 2.2) with the standard work documents that will be introduced in Chapter 5.

In the Check phase of the process, we establish the repeatability of our new standard by making an independent trial (Step 3.1). As appropriate, we verify measurement systems and any critical characteristics associated with patient safety or quality (Steps 3.2 and 3.3).

In the Act/Adhere phase, we write standards using the standard work instruction (Step 4.1). Next, we systematically deploy the new standards (Step 4.2) by training everyone who is required to follow the new standard work. An example of a standard work instruction sheet is shown in Figure 4.9. Instructions for filling out this form are included in Section 5.6 in Chapter 5. It is shown here to provide an example of how to communicate the new standard so that 100 percent adherence is attained. The detail is important if everyone is to understand exactly what the standard is. Examples of applications of standardization and improvements to standard operations are given in Chapter 6.

Finally, we end where we began by using the 5Ss and visual controls to promote adherence to the new standards (Step 4.3).

rona consulting group — operator standard work instruction

Title: Hourly rounds of nurses	Date: December 2010
Departments who must adopt: Hospital	Operators who must adopt: Nurses in care of hospital patients

Task #	Task description (including handoff to appropriate staff to complete task)	Task Time
1	Wash hands before entering room. Tools/supplies: soap, water.	30 sec
2	Greet patient and confirm identity. Tools/supplies: patient ID band, patient chart, intake forms.	30 sec
3	Perform assessment. Tools/supplies: pressure cuff, stethoscope, thermometer.	120 sec
4	Administer medications. Tools/supplies: syringe.	150 sec
5	Wash hands and glove. Tools/supplies: soap, water, gloves.	30 sec
6	Change dressings. Tools/supplies: bandages, medications.	150 sec
7	Deglove and wash hands. Tools/supplies: soap, water.	30 sec
8	Chart at bedside. Tools/supplies: chart, pencil	150 sec
9	Conduct 5S activities, being careful to address potential sources of MRSA. Tools/supplies: saniwipes.	120 sec
10		
11		
12		

Takt time: ***900 seconds/patient***	*Cycle time:* (enter observed cycle time or sum task times)	***810 sec***

NOTE: Pictures showing the appropriate actions in sequence and by step are strongly encouraged. Attach as needed.

Sponsor/process owner: CNO	Origin: Kaizen workshop	Version number: 2

 Page 1 of 1

FIGURE 4.9 Standard work instruction sheet. (Reprinted with permission. J. Michael Rona and Associates, LLC, doing business as Rona Consulting Group © 2008–2011 ©. All rights reserved. http://www.ronaconsulting.com.)

4.5.3 A Review of the Process Analysis Tools

Throughout the standardization improvement process, you will need to use quality control (QC) tools to analyze your data. Figure 4.10 offers a review of these tools and shows at what stage in the improvement process you are most likely to need them.

> **TAKE FIVE**
>
> Take five minutes to think about these questions and write down your answers:
>
> 1. What is the importance of going to the work site to study problems?
> 2. What must you do before establishing a new standard?

QC Tools	Identify problems	Study current conditions (problem identification)	Infer causes	Check to verify causes	Brainstorm improvement plans	Evaluate and select improvement plans	Test improvement plans	Evaluate and verify effects	Standardize improvements	General use	Additional checkpoints for good ideas—improvement methods
1. Graphs	○	◉	○	○				◉	○	For gaining a temporal picture of changes and for making comparisons	Set standards and targets, then study causes of any deviation that occurs and make corrective improvement.
2. Histograms	○	◉						○		For understanding variations in data	Use the 5M categories to find the causes of variation. Then take the same approach described above.
3. Pareto diagrams	◉	○		○				○		For understanding which problems are most important	Use a check sheet along with the Pareto diagram. Take countermeasures that address the most significant problems.
4. Cause-and-effect diagrams		○	◉		○					For analyzing and identifying the causes of problems and methods of controlling them	Use the 5M categories and repeatedly ask "Why?" to gather facts while filling out the diagram.
5. Check sheets		○						○	◉	Facilitates the gathering and organization of data	Same as for Pareto diagrams.
6. Data stratification	◉	◉		◉				○		For grouping data to clarify differences	Set standard values, then investigate differences and their causes.
7. Scatter diagrams	○	○		◉						For studying targeted factors	Repeatedly ask "Why?" to clarify relationships among factors.
8. Control charts	○	○						○	◉	For understanding abnormal data trends	Study data trends as a time series to identify preventable causal factors.

QC Steps

◉ = Very useful   ○ = Useful

FIGURE 4.10 The quality control (QC) tools and their uses. (Reproduced from *Standard Work for the Shopfloor*, p. 30, Productivity Press, New York, 2002. With permission.)

SUMMARY

Standardization includes the following three aspects: the path to reliable methods, 100 percent adherence to reliable methods, and creating and maintaining improvements to standards. These all relate to the process of creating high-quality products at the lowest cost and in the shortest time.

Reliable methods result from authority or custom, data derived from scientific methods, and technical specifications. The first two are changeable standards in healthcare processes. The third refers to quality standards that rarely change.

Whether standards are process or service oriented, standardization depends on communication of the standard for 100 percent adherence to be achieved. Adherence to standards is the key to a strong improvement culture. *It is critical that you communicate the standards simply and easily so that everyone knows what they are and can follow them.* Good standards manuals are hard to come by. Often, the information in manuals is obscure or hard to find. Manuals should include descriptions that are easy to understand, in language that conforms to the standards and conventions of each healthcare organization. Standards formats should be adaptable so that only slight revisions to the manuals are required when service models or processes change. Information in manuals should be clearly oriented to its primary objective: maintaining high service quality and clinical performance.

Standards manuals should include only those items that must be adhered to by everyone. Items that do not need to be checked frequently can be moved to separate standards sheets or manuals. Items that need to be checked often should be positioned in each work area in clear, easy-to-read formats, using as much visual information as possible.

The creation of standards and establishing standardization are important steps in any systematic continuous improvement activity. You must set up a spiral of improvement in standard operations that becomes an integral part of daily work.

Standardization is not only adherence to standards but also the continual creation of new and better standards.

First, you identify and describe the problems. Then you organize the data you have gathered and determine the relative advantage of solving each problem. Next, choose the problem you want to address first, set a target for improvement, and then investigate causes. It is essential that you actually go to the work site and closely examine the operation or process being improved so that you do not make incorrect assumptions about the actual causes. Once you have examined the problem carefully, draw and describe the current conditions in detail, and then brainstorm solutions. Test some of them until you find the best one. After running the final solution through the process and checking that the problem is solved permanently, you are ready to establish this new standard and communicate it to everyone.

The standardization process is designed to help you identify the things you are doing to make up for problems in the process. By doing this you will be able to find permanent solutions to the aggravating and persistent difficulties you have been facing every day. If you think of standards and standardization as a one-time thing—fixed and never to be changed—then you will miss the advantage of standardization as a continual learning and improving mechanism for making your workday happier and easier for clinicians and support staff, and safer for patients. The standardization improvement cycle can become a meaningful and rewarding part of your everyday work.

REFLECTIONS

Now that you have completed this chapter, take five minutes to think about these questions and write down your answers:

1. What did you learn from reading this chapter that stands out as particularly useful or interesting?
2. Do you have any questions about the topics presented in this chapter? If so, what are they?
3. What additional information do you need to understand fully the ideas presented in this chapter?

Chapter 5

Standard Work

Key Point

In Chapter 2, we stated that, like all Lean production methods, standard work maximizes performance and minimizes the seven wastes (see Figure 2.2). In Chapter 3, we stated that standard work was a tool used to allocate worker and process time in proportion to patient demand. *Standard work defines the most reliable work procedures and sequences for each process and operation so that clinicians and staff members can easily change positions within the process as needed to meet current patient demand.* Standard work describes individual procedures, their sequence, and their timing to meet patient demand with the most effective deployment of clinicians and support staff.

Standard work involves five important tasks as shown in Figure 5.1:

1. Standard task
2. Standard sequence
3. Standard time
4. Standard work in process
5. Standard work documentation

5.1 STANDARD TASK

Definition

A task is an individual assignment of work in a single operation or cycle of work. A standard task is a task performed in the same way every time, no matter who performs it—and no matter where they went to medical school or nursing school.

Key Point

On the shop floor of healthcare, standard tasks are necessary building blocks of evidence-based practice. This is not to say that there is no room for discretion in medicine or in healthcare generally. It is to say, however,

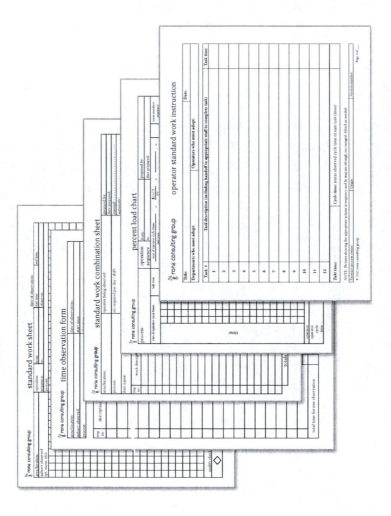

FIGURE 5.1 Standard work documents. (Reprinted with permission. J. Michael Rona and Associates, LLC, doing business as Rona Consulting Group © 2008–2011 ©. All rights reserved. http://www.ronaconsulting.com.)

that where the evidence shows that standardization increases patient safety and the quality of clinical outcomes, or that costs can be reduced without compromising safety or quality, tasks should be standardized.

Key Point Standard tasks also help to build a framework for the further scientific investigation of clinical operations and processes. If tasks are not standardized, or if standard tasks are not normally performed as prescribed, then it will be very difficult to study the causes of adverse events or poor clinical outcomes. Measurement—so necessary to scientific inquiry—is enabled by standardization because defects are defined as *deviations* from standards. Thus, an environment that is not defined by adherence to standard tasks is an environment in which scientific inquiry is hardly possible.

5.2 STANDARD WORK SEQUENCE

Definition Standard work sequence is the order of work tasks involved in an operation or the order of operations in a process to complete a cycle of work.

Key Point Although most people like to do things their own way, we may not stop to realize the consequences of not standardizing the order in which we do things. However, it only takes a moment of reflection to understand how important that strict order in a process can be. No one, for example, would consider baking the ingredients of a cake before combining them or getting dressed before taking a shower in the morning. Beyond the obvious cause-and-effect relationships imbedded in process order, standard sequences of tasks also aid in problem solving. We can determine that there are in fact cause-and-effect relationships in the order of tasks only if we normally perform these tasks in a prescribed order. We can then test for cause-and-effect relationships by changing the order and then comparing results. Without imposing a standardized sequence, it becomes impossible to test for causality. Moreover, when things go wrong, if tasks are not performed in the standard order, it is difficult to determine the precise order in which the tasks were performed, and again it becomes difficult to determine exactly what happened or why.

TAKE FIVE

Take five minutes to think about these questions and write down your answers:

1. If you experiment with your work area to determine the ideal work sequence for two clinicians or staff members versus three clinicians or staff members, what changes?
2. How many clinicians or staff members typically work in your work area? Does any work area frequently have idle time? Is any work area overworked or bottle-necked on a regular basis?
3. How many patients do you usually have waiting in your waiting rooms? In your hallways?

5.3 STANDARD TIME

It may seem odd to include a discussion about time in a book on the standardization of healthcare. Where patient safety is concerned, should we not take all the time we need? Yes and no. To return to the cooking analogy introduced earlier, time is clearly important. Once the ingredients for your cake have been properly combined, and in the right order, it is time to put the cake in the oven—but not for an indefinite period. The cake must bake until it is done—not a minute more, not a minute less. In addition, most people know that, while long showers can be relaxing, they can also dry out your skin. Likewise, in healthcare, things should be done in the right amount of time. It is important to realize that standard times in healthcare are not driven by artificially imposed efficiency targets. These times are arrived at first by studying patient demand and then by experimenting with the process to discover and perhaps to improve its actual capacity.

There are several terms used to describe and calculate the rate of production of healthcare services. They are often confused or misunderstood. Following are definitions and applications of the different terms to help you keep them straight.

50

5.3.1 Takt Time

Definition

Takt time is the average rate at which healthcare services must be provided to meet the demand for services based upon patient requirements. In a Lean healthcare system, takt time is the rhythm of service production in harmony with the volume and mix of patient requirements. It is a calculated time that sets the pace of healthcare service production by clinicians and support staff. To determine takt time, divide available production time by the rate of patient demand. If demand is 120 units per day and there are 480 minutes of operating time per day, then takt time is 4 minutes. If patients want only four procedures per month, takt time is one week. As you can see, takt time is not a measure of how many procedures you are capable of performing but how many you must perform to meet demand.

Takt time fluctuates with the availability of resources (and time) and the level of patient demand. Therefore, it is recalculated whenever there is a change in demand or whenever the number of hours available for service changes. Keeping the flow of service production smooth, departments and work areas balanced, and takt time responsive to actual demand are the new challenges of healthcare production planning. The normally difficult task of predicting healthcare demand is replaced by the possibility of adjusting production daily, and ultimately shift-by-shift or even within a single shift, to meet the needs of a constantly changing patient environment. In fact, takt time has been successfully used to schedule resources in emergency departments, one of the most challenging of all healthcare environments in which to predict what will happen from day to day.

You should understand that takt time is not the time that clinicians or support staff actually spend with each patient, which will vary widely according to the patient, the diagnosis, and the complexity of treatment. Takt time is the average time that a patient will *exit* the healthcare process after being diagnosed and treated, assuming that the process is capable of meeting patient demand within the time available for service.

5.3.2 Cycle Time

Definition

Cycle time is the amount of time it takes for a clinician or staff member to complete one operation or sequence of tasks in a healthcare process, including both value-adding and non-value-adding activities in the work cycle.

Continuous improvement activities address cycle time as one of the most direct ways of eliminating waste. Improving cycle time means eliminating all extraneous, non-value-added activities until the operation is purely value-added, or as close to this as is possible. When the cycle time of an operation is free of waste, the operation has become a reliable, standard method to be standardized throughout the healthcare system.

5.3.3 Wait Time

Definition

Wait time is the time between the end of one operation or work cycle until the beginning of the next operation or cycle. In Figure 2.2, for example, wait times were illustrated by the triangles between work cycles. In the hospital or clinic, wait time is the time patients must wait to be seen or must wait in-between cycles of work. In the lab, wait time is the time lab samples sit before they are processed or in-between laboratory operations.

5.3.4 Lead Time

Definition

Lead time is the sum of all cycle times and wait times for the start of a defined process to the end of that process. For example, in the process of visiting the hospital, lead time is the time from when the patient is admitted until the time he is discharged. The lead time for processing a urine sample is the time from when the doctor writes an order for the sample to be analyzed until the doctor receives results from the lab. Once again in Chapter 2, Figure 2.2, lead time was illustrated by the "castle wall" beneath the process boxes

Key Point and triangles.

TAKE FIVE

Take five minutes to think about these questions and write down your answers:

1. What is the difference between cycle time and takt time?
2. What is lead time?
3. In your opinion, what would be the easiest way to reduce lead time?

5.4 STANDARD WORK-IN-PROCESS (SWIP) INVENTORY

Definition

Standard work-in-process (SWIP) inventory is the minimum amount of "inventory" that is needed for work to progress without creating idle time or interrupting the flow of service production. In the hospital or clinic, our inventory consists of patients in the process; thus, SWIP is the standard number of patients required to keep our clinicians and staff members producing services at takt time. In the lab, inventory consists of lab samples; thus, SWIP is the standard number of samples required to keep lab personnel and equipment producing lab results at takt time.

Continuous improvement of the standards in your process will allow you to reduce SWIP to the minimum buffer.

5.5 STANDARD WORK DOCUMENTATION

The implementation of standard work is a rigorous, scientific, and well-documented process of observation, experimentation, and checking of results. In Figure 5.1, we see the five classic pieces of standard work documentation. Each offers a different "lens" or point of view that helps to bring the work into focus. Each document is introduced briefly here and then discussed at length in Section 5.6 as it relates to one of the five steps to implementing standard work.

1. *Time Observation Form.* The Time Observation Form is used to conduct running time studies of work to determine the actual content of the work and to discover opportunities for improvement.
2. *Standard Work Sheet.* The Standard Work Sheet is used to map the flow of patients, clinicians, medicines, and equipment through the work area.
3. *Percent Load Chart.* The Percent Load Chart uses data recorded on the Time Observation Form to analyze how well the work of multiple clinicians or staff members is balanced.
4. *Standard Work Combination Sheet.* The Standard Work Combination Sheet uses data recorded on the Time Observation Form to analyze the work of individual clinicians and staff members, in particular to highlight the wastes of walking and long setups.
5. *Standard Work Instruction.* The Standard Work Instruction is used to carefully record standard tasks, standard sequences, takt time, and SWIP, together with any safety and quality checks that will be imbedded in the workflow.

5.6 FIVE STEPS TO STANDARD WORK

5.6.1 Step One: Conduct a Running Time Observation

How-to Steps

In Figure 5.2, we see a Time Observation Form, the first of the five standard work documents. In healthcare, although clinicians may know their individual protocols and procedures well, they often do not know the flow of service operations experienced by patients as they are handed off from one clinician to another, from clinicians to the lab, from lab to pharmacy, etc. Thus, the first step in building standard work is to observe the patient's experience by conducting a running time observation using a stopwatch and a Time Observation Form.

The goal of a running time observation is to determine the tasks of the operation and the actual sequence of tasks (in the current state), together with the actual time it takes

Time Observation Form

Area/location: Dermatology						Date of observation: 3/5/10	
Subject observed: RN						Start time: 9:15 am	
Process: Intake/assessmt						Observer: T. Brown	

Step no.	Description of operation	Observation time					Mode (most freq. occurring) task time	Remarks
		Observations						
		1	2	3	4	5		
1	Walk to front desk/registration area	0:00 / 0:09	0:00 / 0:11	0:00 / 0:10			0:10	
2	Retrieve pt's chart & intake forms	0:09 / 0:07	0:11 / 0:08	0:10 / 0:07			0:07	
3	Walk to waiting area	0:16 / 0:05	0:19 / 0:05	0:17 / 0:04			0:05	
4	Call pt name ×2	0:21 / 0:06	0:24 / 0:04	0:21 / 0:04			0:04	
5	Wait while pt approaches	0:27 / 0:29	0:28 / 0:30	0:25 / 0:15			0:30	
6	Greet pt	0:56 / 0:04	0:58 / 0:05	0:40 / 0:06			0:05	
7	Walk to Tx room, set down ppwk, sit	1:00 / 0:18	1:03 / 0:19	0:46 / 0:17			0:18	
8	Open chart/review	1:18 / 0:07	1:22 / 0:08	1:03 / 0:09			0:08	
9	Interview: ask pt questions, write in chart	1:25 / 3:10	1:30 / 3:14	1:12 / 3:18			3:14	
10	Realize missing a form: walk to front desk to retrieve	4:35 / 0:10	4:44 / 0:10	4:30			0:10	3rd obs: was not missing form
11	Look for form/find	4:45 / 0:07	4:54 / 0:07	4:30			0:08	
12	Walk back to room/sit	4:52 / 0:10	5:01 / 0:10	4:30			0:10	
13	Continue interview	5:02 / 2:30	5:11 / 2:26	4:30 / 2:15			2:26	
14	Walk to sink	7:32 / 0:03	7:37 / 0:03	6:45 / 0:03			0:03	
15	Wash hands/put on gloves	7:35 / 0:14	7:40 / 0:15	6:48 / 0:16			0:15	
16	Walk to pt	7:49 / 0:03	7:55 / 0:03	7:04 / 0:03			0:03	
17	Examine wound/lesions, talk to pt	7:52 / 0:24	7:58 / 0:25	7:07 / 0:30			0:25	
18	Walk to sink	8:16 / 0:03	8:23 / 0:03	7:37 / 0:04			0:03	
19	Remove gloves/wash hands	8:19 / 0:10	8:26 / 0:11	7:41 / 0:12			0:11	

FIGURE 5.2 Time observation form. (Reprinted with permission. J. Michael Rona and Associates, LLC, doing business as Rona Consulting Group © 2008–2011 ©. All rights reserved. http://www. ronaconsulting.com.)

to perform each task. Without this knowledge, we cannot ensure that clinical and supporting resources are matched to actual demand, nor can we staff our operations with the appropriate number of people or mix of skills, nor can we confidently plan for improvement. Normally, a running time observation requires us to list each work task in a work cycle before we begin observation. We simply start a stopwatch at the beginning of the process, and then as each task in the cycle is completed we record on the Time Observation Form the elapsed time as it appears on the stopwatch. The stopwatch continues to run until we have observed each task in the cycle. Later, we calculate individual times for each task in the cycle. This information will be used to construct Percent Load Charts (see Figure 5.6) and Standard Work Combination Sheets (see Figure 5.7), which will guide the process of standardization and improvement.

Unfortunately, healthcare operations can often be very untidy and there may not even be a standard sequence of tasks. Therefore, it may not be possible to list all tasks in a given work cycle in sequence before we begin our time observation. In this case, patience must be exercised, as tasks in a work cycle cannot be listed until we observe them actually being performed. For this reason, running time studies can take more time in healthcare than in industries such as manufacturing, where historically a higher degree of standardization is the norm. It is important to observe each task of the work cycle regardless of the sequence of tasks. So persevere until you are reasonably certain that you have seen all that there is to see, regardless of what may feel like false starts or dead ends. Complete the Time Observation Form as follows:

1. Preparation. Meet with people in the workplace and explain what you are doing and why you are doing it.
   a. Inform clinicians and staff members that you are conducting the study to find a safer, better, easier way to perform the work.
   b. When you arrive at the work area, inform patients that you are conducting the study to find a safer, better, easier way to provide care.
   c. Ask clinicians and staff members to work at the normal pace while the timing is being done.
   d. Observe the operation for a couple of cycles to identify the work tasks (if they are not already clear) and determine the start and stop point of work each cycle.

2. Header information. Complete the header of the form (from left to right).
   a. Area/location. Enter the name of the work area or location of the time observation.
   b. Date of observation. Enter the date of the study.
   c. Subject observed. Enter the name of the subject observed (i.e., clinician, staff member, or patient).
   d. Start time. Enter the time that the study was begun.
   e. Process/operation. Enter the name of the process or operation you observed.*
   f. Observer. Enter the name of the person conducting the study.
3. In the body of the Time Observation Form.
   a. Preparation. Conduct an initial time observation to understand the flow of work and to identify the tasks and sequence of tasks. Hold the stopwatch and make observations of elapsed time for at least three cycles. Record the time in pencil on the Time Observation Form, which should be secured on a clipboard.
   b. Task no. In the two left-hand columns of the Time Observation Form, list and number the tasks or steps of work in this work cycle. If the work cycle is already standardized, make this list before starting the formal time observation. Otherwise, list and number the tasks during the time observation.
   c. Description of task. Briefly describe each task you have identified.
   d. Observation time. Conduct a running time observation to gather information about each work task (four to five times). Reset the stopwatch to zero. Enter a zero next to task number 1 in the upper row of the third column from the left under the number

---

* In healthcare, we sometimes use the Time Observation Form to support value stream mapping, in which case we follow a patient through numerous healthcare operations that add up to an entire process (please refer again to Figure 2.2 in Chapter 2). Traditionally, however, the Time Observation Form has been used mainly to study the individual operations in a process, and it is very often used this way in healthcare, too, when we study the flow of clinicians and support staff, medicines, and supplies.

"1." Then start the watch when the operation begins and *do not stop the watch until all observations are complete*. Be careful to observe when the staff member finishes one work task and begins another. In the column corresponding to your observation, record the *elapsed* times that you have observed in the upper cells corresponding to the tasks observed. Leave the lower cells blank for now.

e. Remarks. For each work task, record any problems observed at the far right-hand side of the Time Observation Form in the "Remarks" column.

f. Return to the training room and do the math:

　i. Calculate the time required for a given task by subtracting the start time for that task (in the upper box in the numbered observation column corresponding to that task) from the start time for the next task (in the upper box in the numbered column corresponding to the next task observed).

　ii. Record the task time in the lower box corresponding to each task.

　iii. Total the task times for each cycle of observations and enter the number at the bottom of each column. These numbers are the observed cycle times for the operation.

　iv. Circle the most common time for each task and record it in the "most common time" column. If there is no clear pattern, eliminate the obvious highs and lows and average the remaining observations.

　v. Add the times in the most common task time column. Make sure the number matches the number you circled in Step 10. If not, time any tasks not measured yet. Review times with the team.

4. Footer information.

　a. Version. Enter the version number.

　b. Approved by. Enter the name of the manager who approved the study.

c. Sponsors. Enter the name or names of the managers who sponsored the study.

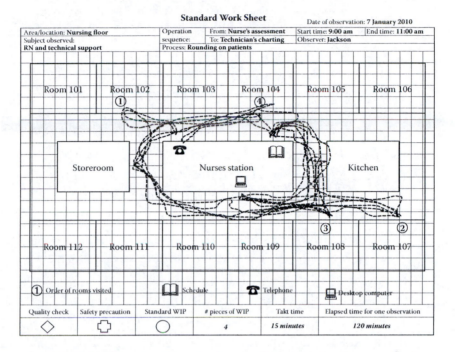

Standard Work Sheet			Date of observation: **7 January 2010**	
Area/location: **Nursing floor**	Operation sequence:	From: **Nurse's assessment**	Start time: **9:00 am**	End time: **11:00 am**
Subject observed:		To: **Technician's charting**	Observer: **Jackson**	
RN and technical support	Process: **Rounding on patients**			

Room 101   Room 102 ①   Room 103   Room 104 ④   Room 105   Room 106

Storeroom   ☎ Nurses station 📖 💻   Kitchen ③ ②

Room 112   Room 111   Room 110   Room 109   Room 108 ③   Room 107 ②

① Order of rooms visited	📖 Schedule	☎ Telephone	💻 Desktop computer

Quality check	Safety precaution	Standard WIP	# pieces of WIP	Takt time	Elapsed time for one observation
◇	✚	◯	*4*	*15 minutes*	*120 minutes*

FIGURE 5.3 Standard work sheet. (Reprinted with permission. J. Michael Rona and Associates, LLC, doing business as Rona Consulting Group © 2008–2011 ©. All rights reserved. http://www. ronaconsulting.com.)

5.6.2 Step Two: Create a Standard Work Sheet

The Standard Work Sheet provides an illustration of the process in a particular work area with the layout of equipment, furniture, medicines, and supplies. It is created at the same time that you conduct your running time observation. It includes cycle time, work sequence, SWIP inventory, and any other information on standards in that work area. To ensure adherence to the standards, this chart should be displayed prominently in the work area and clinicians or staff members should check it frequently. Complete the Standard Work Sheet (see Figure 5.3) as follows:

How-to Steps

1. Preparation. Meet with people in the workplace and explain what you are doing and why you are doing it.
2. Header information. Complete the header of the form (from left to right).

a. Area/location. Enter the name of the work area or location of the time observation.
b. Operation sequence:
   i. From: Enter the name of the first task.
   ii. To: Enter the name of the last task.
c. Start time. Enter the time that the study was begun.
d. End time. Enter the time that the study was completed.
e. Date of observation. Enter the date of the study.
f. Subject observed. Enter the name of the subject observed (i.e., clinician, staff member, or patient).
g. Process/operation. Enter the name of the process or operation you observed.
h. Observer. Enter the name of the person conducting the study.

3. In the body of the Standard Work Sheet.
   a. Draw the physical layout. It the layout is too spread out, obtain a facilities map of the area or use multiple sheets to document the area.
   b. Number the tasks on the layout. Connect the tasks with solid lines. Show the return path from the last task back to the first with a dashed line (- - - - - - -).
   c. Identify "touch points" or hand-offs for ease of timing.
   d. Draw a circle (O) to indicate SWIP at machine/processes involved. Raw material and finished products are not included.
   e. Quality checks: Draw a diamond (◇) at each task requiring a quality check.
   f. Safety precautions: Draw a cross (+) at each task requiring special caution.

4. Footer information.
   a. # pieces of WIP. Enter the amount of SWIP for the operation.
   b. Takt time. Enter the takt time for the operation.
   c. Elapsed time for one observation. Enter the elapsed time in minutes for the duration of the study.
   d. Version. Enter the version number.

e. Approved by. Enter the name of the manager who approved the study.

f. Sponsors. Enter the name or names of the managers who sponsored the study.

5.6.3 Step Three: Percent Load Chart

Definition

The Percent Load Chart takes the information from the Time Observation Form and displays it visually to determine how many clinicians and support staff are needed in each work area to redistribute work so that takt time can be met (see Figure 5.4). The redistribution of work is called level loading. Level loading ensures that clinicians and support staff are utilizing their respective skill sets to the highest level of their licensure, that idle time does not occur, and that some clinician or staff members are doing neither too much nor too little. This process to achieve full work has been defined clearly in many of the Lean Tools for Healthcare Series books and is summarized in the following.

How-to Steps

Complete the Percent Load Chart as follows:

1. Preparation. Meet with people in the workplace and explain what you are doing and why you are doing it.
2. Header information. Complete the header of the form (from left to right).
   a. Process/operation. Enter the name of the process or operation you observed.
   b. Area/location. Enter the name of the work area or location of the time observation.
   c. Operation sequence:
      i. From: Enter the name of the first task.
      ii. To: Enter the name of the last task.
   d. Observer. Enter the name of the person conducting the study.
   e. Date of observation. Enter the date of the study.
   f. Sum of operator cycle times. Referring to the supporting Time Observation Forms, add up the "most frequently observed" cycle times for all clinicians

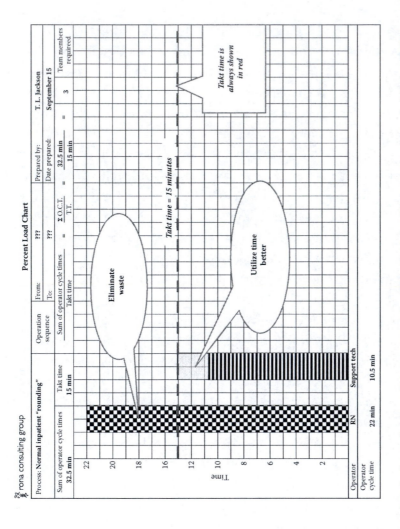

FIGURE 5.4 Percent load chart (before improvement). (Reprinted with permission. J. Michael Rona and Associates, LLC, doing business as Rona Consulting Group © 2008–2011 ©. All rights reserved. http://www.ronaconsulting.com.)

and support staff involved in this operation and enter the total here.

g. Takt time. Enter the takt time for the operation.

h. Team members required. Divide the sum of operator cycle times [the number entered under (f)] by the takt time [entered under (g)] and enter the dividend here.

3. In the body of the Percent Load Chart.

a. Using the Time Observation Forms that you completed in your supporting time studies, calculate each operator's cycle time. For each clinician or staff member, draw a vertical bar to represent his or her cycle time. Based upon your value/non-value add analysis of each clinician or staff member's cycle time, you may color code value adding time and non-value adding time in different colors.

b. With a red pen, draw a horizontal line across the width of the chart to illustrate takt time. Some clinicians' or staff members' bars may extend above the takt time line. This means that those individuals are not normally able to complete all their tasks within the cycle time because they have been assigned too many tasks or some assigned tasks add no value.

c. Operator. Enter the position or level of licensure for the clinician or staff member included in the study.

d. Operator cycle time. Enter the "most frequently recurring" cycle time for the clinician or staff member.

4. Footer information.

a. Version. Enter the version number.

b. Approved by. Enter the name of the manager who approved the study.

c. Sponsors. Enter the name or names of the managers who sponsored the study.

When the Percent Load Chart is complete, use it to analyze and improve the distribution and flow of work by applying the **ECRS** method to:

- **E**liminate non-value-adding tasks that you identified on your current state Percent Load Chart.
- **C**ombine or **c**o-locate related tasks, **c**ross-train (where licensure permits).
- **R**ebalance work by **r**edistributing tasks, **r**esequencing work, or **r**earranging the physical layout.
- **S**implify everything.

Once you have completed your ECRS analysis, create a future state Percent Load Chart to analyze your improvements. An example of a future state Percent Load Chart appears in Figure 5.5. The future state Percent Load Chart verifies mathematically and visually that all clinicians and staff members can comfortably meet takt time (the vertical bars for each clinician or staff member should not cross the red takt time line). Of course, you must test the new work balance by conducting another time observation with stopwatches and Time Observation Forms to confirm your future state percent load. The Percent Load Chart in Figure 5.5 is based upon the Time Observation Forms that appear in Figures 4.9 and 5.3.

Once you have completed and documented your time observations and confirmed your future state Percent Load Chart, recalculate the number of clinicians and staff members required for the operation according to the formula: operators required = the sum of operator cycle times/ by takt time. If you discover that you have too many operators involved in the work in the current state, redeploy some of them to other operations to perform relatively more value-adding tasks. In the case of Figure 5.5, we have begun and ended with two staff members. At first, it seemed that we were understaffed, but now that we have removed the non-value-added waste and rebalanced the work, we can easily meet takt time with the same number of operators.

For a more complete visual explanation of this example, see Chapter 6, Section 6.2.3.

5.6.4 Step Four: Create a Standard Work Combination Sheet

The purpose of the Standard Work Combination Sheet illustrated in Figure 5.6 is to identify opportunities to improve the work of

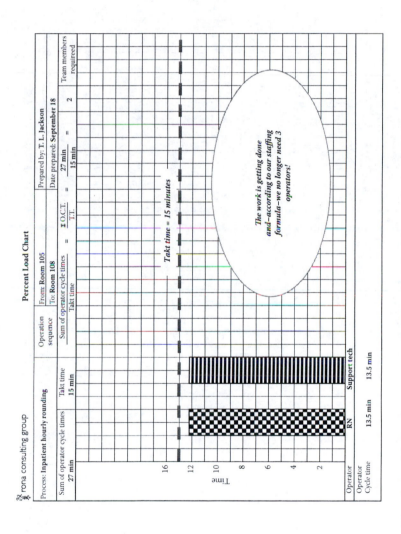

FIGURE 5.5   Percent load chart (after improvement). (Reprinted with permission. J. Michael Rona and Associates, LLC, doing business as Rona Consulting Group © 2008–2011 ©. All rights reserved. http://www.ronaconsulting.com.)

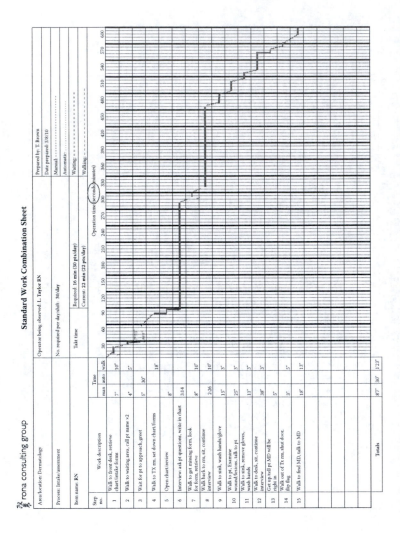

FIGURE 5.6 Standard work combination sheet. (Reprinted with permission. J. Michael Rona and Associates, LLC, doing business as Rona Consulting Group © 2008–2011 ©. All rights reserved. http://www.ronaconsulting.com.)

individual clinicians or staff members. While the Percent Load Chart allows us to see opportunities for improving the work of a *team* of clinicians and staff members, the Standard Work Combination Sheet permits us to see opportunities for improving the work of each *individual* on the healthcare delivery team. So, while the Percent Load Chart helps us to redistribute the work to promote a balanced pace of work, the Standard Work Combination Sheet is an indispensable tool in helping individual clinicians and staff members actually meet takt time by eliminating unnecessary walking, reducing long setups, and resequencing the work in a more rational way.

The Standard Work Combination Sheet takes the information from the Time Observation Form and displays it visually to highlight opportunities for improving the sequence of work tasks by showing the relationship of "manual" time and "machine" time in terms of the total process. "Manual" time is the time clinicians and support staff spend performing specific tasks or work tasks in the work cycle. For purposes of healthcare, "machine" time may refer to the cycling of healthcare equipment (e.g., a dialysis machine or a diagnostic testing machine), or it may refer to the operation of a medicine. Alternatively, it can also refer to "healing time," that is, the time required by the regenerative processes of the human body. The times incorporated on the Standard Work Combination Sheet also include setup time and walking time (see Figure 5.7). Complete this chart as follows:

How-to Steps

1. Preparation. Meet with people in the workplace and explain what you are doing and why you are doing it.
2. Header information. Complete the header of the form (from left to right).
   a. Area/location. Enter the name of the work area or location of the time observation.
   b. Subject observed. Enter the name of the subject observed (i.e., clinician, staff member, or patient).
   c. Observer. Enter the name of the person who made the observations and prepared the sheet.
   d. Process/operation. Enter the name of the process or operation you observed.

e. No. required per day/shift. Enter the number of patients who must be seen, the number of lab samples that must be processed, etc. per day or shift.

f. Licensure. Enter the position or level of licensure of the subject observed.

g. Takt time.

   i. Required. Enter the actual takt time based upon the average demand and time available for providing healthcare services.

   ii. Current. Enter the current cycle time for the operation, which may be larger than takt time.

3. In the body of the Standard Work Combination Sheet:

a. Task no. Enter the number of each task you describe.

b. Task description. Briefly describe each task in the process.

c. Time. Draw a solid, vertical red line indicating current takt time.

4. Enter numbers indicating the sequence of operations/tasks.

5. Enter the actual tasks performed by the operator. Use present tense verb and its direct object (e.g., press button). Enter machine numbers if available.

6. Time. Referring to the supporting Time Observation Form, enter observed times for:

a. Man = Manual Work Time. Enter the time for worker tasks.

b. Auto = Machine Time. Enter the time for tasks performed by equipment or medicines.

c. Walk = Walking Time. Enter the time it takes the clinician or staff member to move to the next station in the work area to touch the patient, wash hands, chart, pick up or put down supplies or instruments, etc.

7. Using a legend, draw the chart to illustrate the simultaneous states of the clinician or staff member, equipment, or (where appropriate) patient.

a. Manual = ---------------------

b. Automatic = ...

c. Waiting = ============

d. Walk = Walking ~~~~~~~~

8. Totals. Add column totals for "man," "auto," and "walk."
9. Footer information.
   a. Version. Enter the version number.
   b. Approved by. Enter the name of the manager who approved the study.
   c. Sponsors. Enter the name or names of the managers who sponsored the study.

5.6.5 Step Five: Standard Work Instruction Sheet

Figure 5.7 details the process at each workstation, providing explicit instructions for new workers so that they will pick

rona consulting group   operator standard work instruction

Title: Hourly rounds of support technicians		Date: December 2010
Departments who must adopt: Hospital	Operators who must adopt: Support technicians who support nurses in care of hospital patients	

Task #	Task description (including handoff to appropriate staff to complete task)	Task time
1	Wash hands before entering room. Tools/supplies: soap, water.	30 sec
2	Greet patient and confirm identity. Tools/supplies: patient ID band, patient chart, intake forms.	30 sec
3	Wash hands and then glove. Tools/supplies: soap, water, gloves.	30 sec
4	Toilet the patient. Tools/supplies: n/a.	150 sec
5	Deglove and wash hands. Tools/supplies: soap, water.	30 sec
6	Reposition the patient. Tools/supplies: n/a.	120 sec
7	Provide personal services as required: brush hair, clip nails, make-up, etc. Tools/supplies: brush, nail clippers, etc.	150 sec
8	Chart at bedside. Tools/supplies: patient chart, pencil.	120 sec
9	Conduct 5S activities, being careful to address potential sources of MRSA. Tools/supplies: saniwipes.	150 sec
10		
11		
12		
Takt time: 900 seconds/patient	Cycle time: (enter observed cycle time or sum task times)	810 sec

NOTE: Pictures showing the appropriate actions in sequence and by step are strongly encouraged. Attach as needed.

Sponsor/process owner: CNO	Origin: Kaizen workshop	Version number: 2

© 2011 rona consulting group   Page 1of 1

FIGURE 5.7 Standard work instruction sheet. (Reprinted with permission. J. Michael Rona and Associates, LLC, doing business as Rona Consulting Group © 2008–2011 ©. All rights reserved. http://www.ronaconsulting.com.)

up the methods quickly and correctly. Complete the Standard Work Instruction Sheet as follows:

1. Preparation. Meet with people in the workplace and explain that you are documenting standard work to increase patient safety and satisfaction and to make the work easier for clinicians and staff members to remember and perform right the first time.

2. Header information. Complete the header of the form (from left to right).

    a. Title. Enter the title of the standard work instruction. (The title normally identifies the scope of the work and who will perform it.)

    b. Date: Enter the date that the standard work instruction was implemented.

    c. Departments who must adopt: Enter the name or names of the departments within the organization that are required to adopt this standard work.

    d. Operators who must adopt: Enter the names of the positions of clinicians and/or support staff who are required to adopt this standard work.

3. In the body of the Standard Work Instruction:

    a. Task no. Enter the number of each task in the process, in sequence.

    b. Task description. Fully and clearly describe each task to be performed, including any tools, supplies, or job aids required. Highlight quality or safety checks built into the process. The description should be sufficient to conduct an effective in-service training.

    c. Task time. Enter the standard task time (normally in seconds) for each task.

    d. Takt time: Enter the takt time for the operation. *takt time = time available / average demand.*

    e. Cycle time: Enter the observed cycle time or sum all task times.

4. Photographs. Photographs showing the appropriate actions in sequence may be attached to the Standard Work Instruction as needed.

5. Footer information.
   a. Sponsor/process owner: Enter the name or position of the sponsor and/or process owner.
   b. Origin: Record the origin of the standard work (kaizen workshop, 3P workshop, suggestion system, etc.).
   c. Version number. Enter the version or revision number of the standard work.

TAKE FIVE

Take five minutes to think about these questions and write down your answers:

1. How much time do you spend looking for equipment or supplies to do your work?
2. How many miles do you walk in a day just to do your work? (This does not mean distance to lunch or breaks, but actual operation time spent walking.) Put on a pedometer and find out.
3. Can you think of one change you could make to reduce this distance by half?
4. How does the Time Observation Form help you standardize your process?
5. How does the Standard Work Sheet help you standardize your process?
6. How does the Percent Load Chart help you redistribute the work of clinicians and staff members to meet takt time?
7. How does the Standard Work Sheet help you find opportunities to resequence work tasks?
8. How does the Standard Work Instruction Sheet support quality?

5.7 TEN GUIDELINES FOR MAINTAINING AND IMPROVING STANDARD WORK

As we emphasized earlier, standard work is not a static requirement or immutable best practice. In order to accommodate the art as well as the science of healthcare, standards and standard work must evolve. The following are some effective guidelines for maintaining and improving standard work.

1. Establish healthcare operations universally throughout the clinic, hospital, lab, or pharmacy that are completely supported by top management.
2. Make sure everyone understands the importance of standard work—from the Chief Executive Officer to the newest employee.
3. See that process owners and anyone responsible for training others in standard work are confident in and committed to the standard works they teach.
4. Post visual displays to remind everyone of the importance of adhering to the standards.
5. Keep your Standard Work Sheet up to date with any improvements and post it with your Standard Work Instructions so that clinicians and staff members can visually compare their own work to the standards.
6. Bring in a third party to clear up any misunderstandings.
7. Hold process owners responsible for maintaining standard work.
8. Reject the status quo. Also, resist benchmarking mediocrity and avoid adopting best practices before you have tested them. Remember that improvement never ends, and continually look for ways to improve the existing standards.
9. Periodically conduct new time studies using the Time Observation Form and analyze the work with Percent Load Charts and Standard Work Combination sheets to gather new ideas and alert one another to problems as they arise.
10. Systematically pursue the establishment of a new, higher level of standard work.

SUMMARY

Like all Lean healthcare service production methods, standard work maximizes performance and minimizes waste.

Standard work defines the most reliable work procedures and sequences and timing for each process and operation so that patients are always safe and you can easily adjust staffing levels to meet the current flow of patient demand. Standard work involves five important tasks: (1) takt time, (2) standard work sequence, and SWIP inventories of (3) patients, (4) medicines, and (5) supplies.

Standard task refers to the requirement that every task in an operation is performed in the exact same way by each clinician or support staff member.

Standard work sequence is the order of work tasks involved in a work cycle or the order of specific tasks to complete a step in a healthcare process. You should understand that the process sequence and the work sequence might be different depending on the number of clinicians or staff members in a department or work area. If takt time is slowed because of a decrease in patient demand for the service produced in that work area, then a single clinician or staff member may be able to run all operations in the work area and keep up with the takt time, provided that all tasks are within the scope of the clinician's or staff member's licensure. If demand increases, several clinicians or staff members may need to be moved into the work area to keep up with the accelerated takt time.

Standard time refers primarily to takt time, which is the rhythm of healthcare service production in harmony with the volume and mix of patient requirements. There are several terms used to describe and calculate the rate of service production that are important to understand. These include *cycle time, wait time,* and *lead time.*

SWIP inventory is the minimum amount of inventory of patients, medicines, and supplies that is needed for work of healthcare to progress without creating idle time or interrupting the flow of services.

Standard work documentation refers to the five standard documents used to execute the five steps to achieving standard work:

- Step One. Conduct a running time observation with a Time Observation Form.

- Step Two. Map the work area and the process with a Standard Work Sheet.
- Step Three. "Balance the line" by creating a Percent Load Chart.
- Step Four. Identify opportunities to resequence the work by creating a Standard Work Combination Sheet.
- Step Five. Ensure smooth implementation and adherence to standard work by creating a Standard Work Instruction Sheet.

For an example of how these documents work as a system, review Figures 6.7 through 6.11 in Chapter 6.

Improvements in standard work can be focused on many aspects of healthcare operations. Improvements in motion are among the most important changes that can be made in the standardization process.

There are important guidelines for maintaining standard work. It is critical in establishing standard work that the guidelines be universally applied throughout the hospital, clinic, and lab and completely supported by top management. Make sure everyone understands the importance of standard work—from the president to the newest employee. Post visual displays to remind everyone of the importance of adhering to the standards, and systematically pursue the establishment of a new, higher level of standard work.

REFLECTIONS

Now that you have completed this chapter, take five minutes to think about these questions and write down your answers:

1. What did you learn from reading this chapter that stands out as particularly useful or interesting?
2. Do you have any questions about the topics presented in this chapter? If so, what are they?
3. What additional information do you need to understand fully the ideas presented in this chapter?

Chapter 6

Applications of Standardization and Standard Work

6.1 APPLICATIONS OF STANDARDIZATION

When standards exist, a manager's responsibility becomes easier because everyone knows what to do and how to do it. *Standards support the delegation of responsibility.* In Chapter 4, standardization was defined and ways to communicate standards were described in some detail. The process of improving and setting new standards was also described. In this chapter, we offer a number of specific applications of standardization to help you identify improvement targets for specific purposes.

6.1.1 New Employee Training

There are three types of training standards to be considered:

1. Employee-to-employee training
2. Training by clinical specialists or managers
3. Training by visual management

Guidelines for these standards follow.

Employee-to-employee training: This is usually an in-service training, which is a very common system of training used in healthcare organizations. However, to be effective, in-service training requires standardization and the scrutiny of continuous improvement cycles to support adherence to reliable methods. Guidelines are listed for what happens in effective employee-to-employee training.

1. The teaching employee discusses the importance of the operation.
2. Basic points of the operation are covered.
3. Patient and employee safety concerns are described.
4. A hands-on, physical demonstration of each step of the operation is given—not in a classroom but in the area where the work is actually performed, with a clear explanation of how to make the work easier, quicker, and more reliable.
5. After watching the task or work cycle being performed, the trainee describes it and then attempts it under superv sion. Begin with the easier steps until they are perfected, then move on to the more complex steps of the operation.
6. The trainee performs the operation unassisted, with review by the teaching employee when mistakes are made.
7. The new employee is welcomed into the group and invited to join ongoing improvement activities, and perhaps assigned a special problem-solving task.

Training by specialists or managers: Specialists or managers follow similar guidelines for training as in employee-to-employee training. The training should always be hands-on at the worksite, even if fundamentals are covered in a classroom. After mastering the basics, teachers should make sure trainees understand the relevant troubleshooting methods.

Using a Standard Work Validation Checklist to post the training that each employee has completed is a good way for trainers to reward and encourage employees to learn more skills (see Figure 6.1). Clinicians and staff members may also be moved from work area to work area as patient demand and work balancing shifts their responsibilities.

Training by visual management: Visual displays of targets and measures, differences between standards and actual results, and the standard work methods themselves give significant

Standard Work Validation Checklist

Department **Nursing**	Evaluation criteria					By/Initials:	*KR*
	1 Unable to do operation		3 Can do operation independently			By/Initials:	*CV*
Section **5 South**	2 Can do with assistance/need review		4 Can do operation well/Instruct			By/Initials:	*AM*
						By/Initials:	*WB*

Competency / Staff member	Red tag	Location indicator	5S audit	Standard work sheet	Time obervation form	Percent load chart	Std work combo sheet	Std work instruction	Mistake-proofing	Quick setup	Kanban
Patti	4	4	4	4	4	4	3	4	4	4	4
Tom	3	2	1	2	3	1	3	3	1	2	2
Jim	4	3	4	4	3	3	2	4	4	3	3
Erin	4	4	4	3	2	4	3	3	2	4	3
Mike	3	4	3	4	3	4	3	4	3	4	3

FIGURE 6.1 Standard work validation checklist. (Reprinted with permission. J. Michael Rona and Associates, LLC, doing business as Rona Consulting Group © 2008–2011 ©. All rights reserved. http://www.ronaconsulting .com)

feedback on how well clinicians and staff members are adhering to the standards. These displays are posted in work areas so that clinicians and staff members can use them to correct variances and recognize where problems exist. Different uses of visual management aids are shown in Figure 6.2.

TAKE FIVE

Take five minutes to think about these questions and write down your answers:

1. What type of in-service training do you have in your organization? Is top management involved in the training process?
2. Do you have support for multi-skill training? Do you have plans to increase your employees' level of licensure to support multi-skilled operations?
3. What types of visual displays do you have for communicating standards?

6.1.2 Evaluating Improvement Ideas

Key Point

The process of creating standards must also be standardized for effective standards to be developed and followed. In Chapter 4, this process was discussed in detail. One additional aspect of the improvement process worth mentioning here is the method of generating and evaluating new ideas.

There are always a number of ways to solve problems and many improvement plans will emerge as teams begin to analyze their operations. How should they choose the ones to standardize?

First, make sure that all ideas are collected. Figure 6.3 shows an Idea Summary Sheet, which can be used to track and illustrate ideas as they arise in an employee's mind. If all ideas for solving a particular problem are written down and then illustrated, it will be easier for the team to understand the solutions being presented and discuss their value.

Figure 6.4 illustrates a simple Idea Evaluation Chart that maps ideas according to their relative impact and the relative

Management Target	Implementation Items
1. Process management and deadline management	Service production management and scheduling boards (for process control), graphs comparing target values to result values (takt time adherence and capacity utilization), display boards (e.g., for standard work instructions, shift change protocols, and urgent items).
2. Quality control	"Stop the line" guidelines and management telephone numbers, defect graph (rate and trends) for both adherence to evidence-based practice (standard work) and clinical outcomes, display of defect-prevention rules, etc.
3. Healthcare operations management	Healthcare operations standards (technical standards and process standards), skills training achievement chart, bulletin boards for notices regarding causes of interruptions in patient care, improvement campaign results, etc.
4. Materials management	Storage site specifications, names of medicines, supplies, tools, etc. kanban card displays, displays of minimum and maximum allowable inventory, visual floor area and height restrictions for storage areas; defect storage site indicators; notices about missing inventory items, items awaiting disposal, items to be repaired, etc.
5. Management of equipment and facilities	Maintenance schedules and results charts; displays of equipment checkpoints (sections and check items); routine inspection check sheets; storage site instructions for special equipment and tools (including inventory ordering information); spare parts inventory; inventory shelf management; tags indicating name of equipment manager; notices describing reasons for failures or breakdowns etc.
6. Patient and staff safety	Patient and staff safety guidelines and special safety-related notices.
7. Improvement goals and improvement management	Weekly and daily charts showing progress toward improvement targets, staff and equipment capacity utilization results, defect elimination results, work-in-process and inventory trend charts, safety trend charts, 5S activity progress charts, improvement proposal campaign results, displays of improvement case studies, etc.

FIGURE 6.2   Examples of visual management targets and improvement items. (Reproduced from *Standard Work for the Shopfloor*, p. 62, Productivity Press, New York, 2002. With permission.)

cost of implementation (in terms of time and money). Simple charts such as the Idea Evaluation Chart are very effective in the context of traditional 5-day Kaizen workshops, where a team of clinicians and staff members must process a great deal of information quickly. After brainstorming ideas, participants place their Idea Summary Sheets on the chart and discuss their relative value. Ideas that score high in terms of impact and low in terms of cost are often the most effective. Thus, ideas in the upper right-hand corner of the chart are strong candidates for implementation during a week of Kaizen.

Idea Summary Sheet

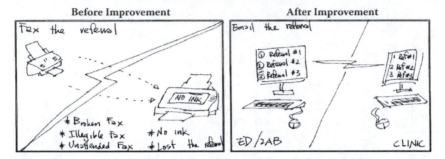

FIGURE 6.3 Idea summary sheet. (Reprinted with permission. J. Michael Rona and Associates, LLC, doing business as Rona Consulting Group © 2008–2011 ©. All rights reserved. http://www.ronaconsulting.com)

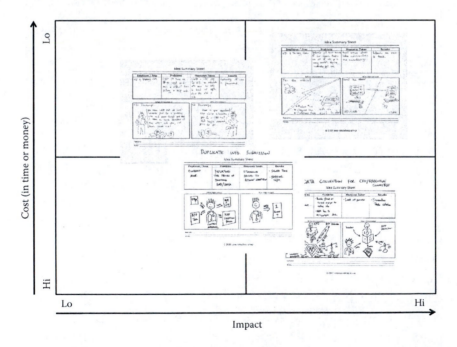

FIGURE 6.4 Idea evaluation chart. (Reprinted with permission. J. Michael Rona and Associates, LLC, doing business as Rona Consulting Group © 2008–2011 ©. All rights reserved. http://www.ronaconsulting.com)

TAKE FIVE

Take five minutes to think about these questions and write down your answers:

1. What are some factors involved in creating quality healthcare services?
2. How do you keep track of ideas for solving problems in your clinics, hospitals, labs, and pharmacies?
3. Do you have a method for evaluating which ideas are best?

TAKE FIVE

Take five minutes to think about these questions and write down your answers:

1. What are a few functions of the process management role?
2. How does Lean healthcare service production simplify process management?

6.2 APPLICATIONS OF STANDARD WORK

At the beginning of this book, we say that standard work is essential to Lean healthcare operations. We hope that by now you understand why. Standards are the foundation of patient safety, quality, and continuous improvement. Without them, you cannot focus or measure your improvements. By the time you have implemented standardization and standard work, everyone should have begun to embrace a culture of continuous improvement. Standards and standard work, as we have shown throughout this book, are not static or unchanging. Standardization and standard work are, in fact, the basis from which improvement changes can be analyzed, and tested and then adopted by everyone systematically. They are the content of training efforts—you train people to adhere to both technical and process standards. Standard work, when implemented, creates an even workload for every employee, so that no one works too little or too much, idle time is reduced, and bottlenecks are eliminated.

6.2.1 Managing Healthcare Service Production Processes

The management of healthcare service production aims to control healthcare service production variables—what, when, where, and how many activities it takes to deliver healthcare services of the highest safety and quality, in the shortest time, and at the lowest costs to the patient. It helps smooth the flow of activities from the presentation of the patient symptoms, to assessment, to diagnosis, to doctors' orders, to the execution of those orders by nurses and support staff. Healthcare service production management can serve a number of purposes, all of which are related to the type of patient and patient requirements being served by the healthcare service. Figure 6.5 shows the functions of healthcare service production management and how to create checkpoints according to the Plan-Do-Check-Act cycle of continuous improvement. It breaks down the management functions into four aspects: planning, testing, implementing, and supervision.

Key Point

In the standardization of healthcare service production management, the methods of Lean production create visual checkpoints throughout the production process for all aspects of the management function so that communication is immediate and universal. Visual displays and controls, mistake-proofing, and quick setup methods continually decrease work-in-process inventory and defects. Clinicians and support staff become their own inspectors of both the process and the technical standards. The ultimate end of Lean healthcare is the ability to implement a healthcare service production system with a high degree of safety and flexibility to respond effectively and appropriately to changes in patient demand.

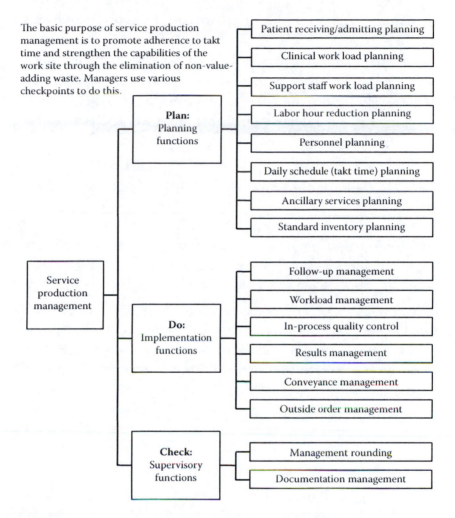

The basic purpose of service production management is to promote adherence to takt time and strengthen the capabilities of the work site through the elimination of non-value-adding waste. Managers use various checkpoints to do this.

Service production management

Plan: Planning functions
- Patient receiving/admitting planning
- Clinical work load planning
- Support staff work load planning
- Labor hour reduction planning
- Personnel planning
- Daily schedule (takt time) planning
- Ancillary services planning
- Standard inventory planning

Do: Implementation functions
- Follow-up management
- Workload management
- In-process quality control
- Results management
- Conveyance management
- Outside order management

Check: Supervisory functions
- Management rounding
- Documentation management

FIGURE 6.5 Service production management functions. (Reproduced from *Standard Work for the Shopfloor*, p. 67, Productivity Press, New York, 2002. With permission.)

6.2.2 Patient Safety

Key Point

In order to ensure patient safety, standard work is an absolutely necessity. Standard work procedures are the basis for integrating quality checks directly into the work process—the ultimate key to patient safety. Standard work enhances patient safety in three vital ways.

First, because standard work is the most reliable way we know how to serve the patient, and because standard work by definition means that we adhere to our standards, we are assured that the right things will be done time and time again.

Second, adherence to standards means that when something does go wrong, we are able to gather good data and create useful information, because defects can only be measured in terms of deviations from standard work. Where there is no standard work or adherence to standards, all data are questionable. We really cannot know what is going on.

Third, an important feature of standard work is that it allows us to build quality checks directly into the work process, and is referenced clearly on the Standard Work Instruction Sheet (see, for example, Figure 5.3 in Chapter 5). Successive checks of previous work ensure that conditions for safety and quality exist before we begin our work. Self-checks of our own work ensure patient safety and quality as the process continues. We can even mistake-proof our work with checklists or physical devices to achieve zero defects. In Figure 6.6, we see the California Pacific Medical Center's Surgical Safety Checklist, a good example of mistake-proofing in action. In the context of standard work, failure to follow such a checklist included on the Standard Work Instruction Sheet would constitute a defect and trigger corrective action.

6.2.3 Hourly Rounding

Key Point

Within the world of inpatient care, the practice of hourly rounding has been identified as a "best practice" that increases patient safety, improves clinical outcomes, and improves employee morale. The evidence behind the practice of hourly rounding indicates that nurse-sensitive indicators such as the frequency of falls and pressure ulcers improve dramatically if once every 60 minutes each patient receives a standard "bundle" of healthcare services including assessment, adjustments in pain medication, assistance in going to the bathroom, etc. Standard work is an excellent way to implement and perhaps improve hourly rounding. Standard work also helps to ensure that all clinicians and support staff will support the new approach.

**California Pacific
Medical Center**
A Sutter Health Affiliate
With You. For Life.

**UNIVERSAL PROTOCOL
PROCEDURAL SAFETY CHECKLIST**
(Conducted in Procedure Room)

Addressograph

TIME OUT: All members of the procedure team are present and actively engaged in the Time Out. The surgeon/proceduralist will initiate the Time Out. The Checklist coordinator will call out each element, ensure each element is addressed, prompt the team for response when needed, and document. The **TIME OUT** confirms the following **(as applicable):**

Item	Time Out #1 (Regional Block or Primary Procedure) (✓ or N/A)	Time Out #2 (as necessary) (✓ or N/A)
All activities are suspended (Members of the care team are expected to speak up immediately and **STOP** the process if they notice any discrepancy or believe any step in the safety check is missed or incomplete.)		
Patient verified using two identifiers		
Correct Procedure (with consent present for verification)		
Correct site/side confirmed		
Site Marking (or alternative process)		
Correct position		
Implants/Special equipment		
Relevant images and results are labeled/displayed		
Known Allergies		
Antibiotic		
Appropriate VTE prophylaxis initiated as indicated		
Are critical events anticipated?		
The signature attests that the time out was performed prior to the start of the procedure with the immediate members of the procedure team, and other active participants as appropriate for the procedure.	Signature/Date/Time	Signature/Date/Time

Nursing Team Reviews:
☐ Sterility indicator results confirmed   ☐ Medication labeling (back table) verified

SIGN OUT (Before Patient Leaves Procedure Area)

Nurse verbally confirms with the team:
☐ Instrument, sponge and needle counts reconciled ☐ N/A
☐ Specimen is labeled; path requisition completed ☐ N/A
☐ Wound class confirmed with surgeon ☐ N/A
☐ Equipment problems to be addressed ☐ N/A

☐ Surgeon/proceduralist, anesthesiologist and nurse review the key concerns for recovery and management of this patient:
Plan for transition of care
Destination
Receiving unit notified
Handoff/communication to receiving unit

Nurse Signature:- **, RN Date:** - - - - - - - - - - **Time:** - - - - - - - - - -

Tab # G (04/10) 7149
OR Intra Op-200088   Distribution: ORIGINAL: to Chart   COPY: to Manager

FIGURE 6.6 California Pacific Medical Center's surgical safety checklist. (Reprinted with permission. Sutter West Bay Hospitals doing business as California Pacific Medical Center © 2009–2011 ©. All rights reserved. http://www.CPMC.org)

Let us assume that a healthcare team consisting of one registered nurse and one qualified support technician is assigned to care for four patients during a shift of eight hours. The work is divided between the nurse and the technician based upon their respective levels of licensure, or so it seems. In fact, no one has actually observed the work or thought through it systematically. Prodded by the organization's chief executive officer, external "Lean consultants'" lead time observation studies resulting in the Percent Load Chart that appears in Chapter 5 as Figure 5.4 (before improvement). We might expect that the nurse's responsibilities include questioning the patient and, based upon the patient's requirements, adjusting pain medications, assisting the patient in going to the bathroom, etc. The technician's responsibilities might include periodically positioning the patient, assisting the patient to and from the bathroom, providing personal care (such as brushing hair or bathing), and other types of services that do not require administration or supervision by a nurse. The nurse's work and the technician's work may be thought of as two "bundles" of care delivered, respectively, by the nurse and technician.

Bundle 1. Nursing bundle—questions, adjustments in pain medication, toileting

Bundle 2. Support technician bundle—questions, toileting, positioning, and personal care

In addition to improvements in nurse sensitive indicators, when hourly rounding is implemented a strange new calm falls over the entire nursing floor. Patient call lights stop blinking, almost entirely. Job satisfaction increases and turnover (very expensive) decreases because nurses and technicians can spend more time at bedside, which is why they entered the profession in the first place.

In Figure 6.7, we see the choreographed delivery of healthcare services by the nurse and support technician. This is accomplished through the implementation of standard work. To restate the "best practice" in terms of standard work, it would appear that the takt time for the process of inpatient rounding is 15 minutes per patient because, based upon the evidence, the average patient demand is one healthcare service bundle per hour. In our example, there are four patients to be served by the team in the available time of 1 hour. Therefore, takt time for four complete (bundle 1 + bundle 2)

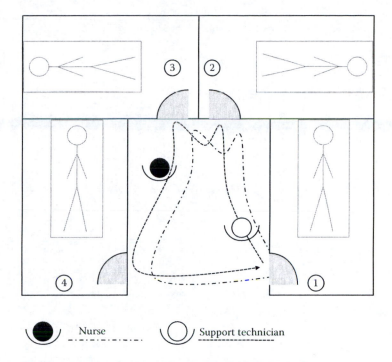

service bundles delivered every 60 minutes is 15 minutes per service bundle. In other words, every 15 minutes a patient will receive the last of two visits, one by the nurse and one by the support technician.

To test the hypothesis posed by this "best practice," the improvement team first constructs a current state Standard Work Sheet to map the flow (or lack of it) in the work of the nurse and the technician. See the "current state" in Figure 6.8. At the same time, the team conducts its own running time observations of the nurse and the technician using Time Observation Forms. See the "current state" in Figure 6.9. Based upon the time observations, the team constructs a current state Percent Load Chart. See the "current state" in Figure 6.10.

Upon analysis of the current state Percent Load Chart, the team discovers that if certain tasks currently performed by the registered nurse are transferred to the support technician and if non-value-adding wastes such as the transport of

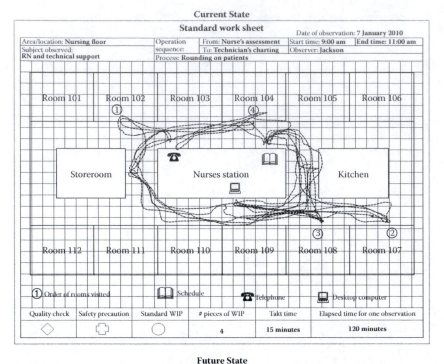

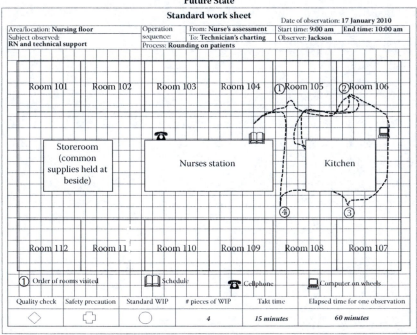

FIGURE 6.8 Current and future state standard work sheets. (Reprinted with permission. J. Michael Rona and Associates, LLC, doing business as Rona Consulting Group © 2008–2011 ©. All rights reserved. http://www.ronaconsulting.com)

Current State

Time observation form

Process: RN rounds	Observation time					Observer: Mary R.		Date: 7-Jan-10
Step no.	description of operation	observations				Shortest	Most common	Remarks
1	Greet patie... identity							
2	Wash hand...							
3	Take phon...							
4	Look for d...							
5	Ask questi...							
6	Adjust pai...							
21	Chart at b...							
22	Conduct 5...							
	time for c...							

Time observation form

Process: Technician rounds	Observation time					Observer: Mary R.		Date: 27-Jan-10
Step no.	Description of operation	Observations					Shortest	Most common	Remarks
		1	2	3	4	5			
1	Greet patient and confirm identity	30					na	30	
2	Walk to store room to retrieve glvoes	180					na	180	
3	Wash hands and glove	30					na	30	
4	Toilet the patient	150					na	150	
5	Deglove and wash hands.						na	30	
6	Walk to the store room to retireve comb	180					na	180	
15	Chart at bedside.	120					na	120	
16	Conduct 5S activities.	150					na	150	
	Time for one cycle	1400						1400	Minimum is target

Future State

Time observation form

Process: RN rounds	Observation time					Observer: Mary R.		Date: 27-Jan-10
Step no.	Description of operation	Observations					Shortest	Most common	Remarks
1	Greet patie... identity								
2	Wash hand...								
3	Toilet the p...								
4	Deglove an...								
5	Reposition...								
6	Provide pe...								
7	Chart at be...								
8	Conduct 5...								
	Time for c...								

Time observation form

Process: Technician rounds	Observation time					Observer: Mary R.		Date: 27-Jan-10
Step no.	description of operation	Observations					Shortest	Most common	Remarks
		1	2	3	4	5			
1	Greet patient and confirm identity	0 / 32	742 / 28	1535 / 29			28	30	
2	Wash hands and glove.	32 / 28	770 / 31	1564 / 30			28	30	
3	Toilet the patient.	60 / 135	801 / 160	1594 / 150			135	150	
4	Deglove and wash hands.	195 / 25	961 / 34	1744 / 33			25	30	
5	Reposition the patient.	220 / 122	995 / 125	1777 / 106			106	120	
6	Provide personal services.	342 / 152	1120 / 155	1883 / 135			135	150	
7	Chart at bedside.	494 / 110	1275 / 115	2018 / 130			110	120	
8	Conduct 5S activities.	604 / 138	1390 / 145	2148 / 160			138	150	
	Time for one cycle	742	793	773				780	Minimum is target

FIGURE 6.9 Current and future state time observation forms. (Reprinted with permission. J. Michael Rona and Associates, LLC, doing business as Rona Consulting Group © 2008–2011 ©. All rights reserved. http://www.ronaconsulting.com)

Current State

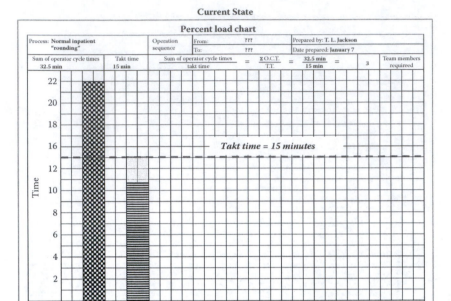

Future State

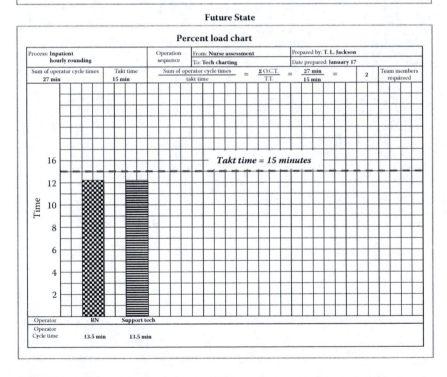

FIGURE 6.10 Current and future state percent load charts. (Reprinted with permission. J. Michael Rona and Associates, LLC, doing business as Rona Consulting Group © 2008–2011 ©. All rights reserved. http://www.ronaconsulting.com)

FIGURE 6.11 Standard work instructions for hourly rounding. (Reprinted with permission. J. Michael Rona and Associates, LLC, doing business as Rona Consulting Group © 2008–2011 ©. All rights reserved. http://www.ronaconsulting.com)

supplies are removed entirely from the workflow, the team of nurse/technician can easily round on four patients every hour. To redesign the work, the team writes Standard Work Instructions for the nurse and the technician (see Figure 6.11). Next, the team constructs a future state Standard Work Sheet (Figure 6.8, "future state") and a future state Percent Load Chart (Figure 6.9, "future state"). Then the team conducts another running time observation with Time Observation Forms to validate the new standard work (Figure 6.10, "future state"). Any adjustments in the work should be recorded on the Standard Work Instructions (Figure 6.11).

6.2.4 Satisfied Employees

Generally, you will discover that everyone resists standardization until they understand what it really means and how it benefits the organization and workers alike. It is often thought that standard procedures will destroy innovation and creativity. People do not want to do their work the same way as everyone else, and they do not want to do it the same way every time. In fact, 100 percent of the time, once standardization is in effect and standard work is in place, creativity, improvement, and job satisfaction increase. Now a system is part of daily work to test and improve the standards. Recognition for making improvements builds self-esteem, and skill levels increase through training for multi-skill work. Training becomes more effective, turnover rates drop, and communication among teams and between shifts increases—people know what they need to know when they need to know it. Only after working in an environment where standard work is in place do you discover the advantages that inevitably result.

Standardization and standard work procedures depend on and derive from all the methods of a Lean healthcare system; they bring these methods to their full potential, and they set in motion a continuous improvement cycle for the whole organization that is never ending.

TAKE FIVE

Take five minutes to think about these questions and write down your answers:

1. What are some advantages to continuous flow?
2. How does standard work support continuous flow?
3. What type of safety checks might be included as part of your standard work?

SUMMARY

In this chapter, we offer a number of specific applications of standardization to help you identify improvement targets for specific purposes: new employee training, evaluating improvement ideas, healthcare service production management, and decision making.

New employee training includes employee-to-employee training, training by specialists or managers, and training by means of visual management. Employee-to-employee, in-service training is the most common system of training used in healthcare. However, to be effective, in-service training requires standardization and the scrutiny of continuous improvement cycles to support adherence to reliable methods. Training by specialists or managers should always be hands-on at the worksite, even if fundamentals are covered in a classroom. After mastering the basics, teachers should make sure trainees understand the relevant troubleshooting methods. Training by means of visual management uses displays of targets and measures, differences between standards and actual results, and the standard work procedures themselves to give feedback on how well operations are adhering to the standards. These displays are posted in the workplace so that employees can easily use them to correct variances and recognize where problems exist.

Healthcare service production management aims to control service production variables—the what, when, where, and how of many discrete activities it takes to deliver healthcare services of the highest safety and quality, in the shortest time, and at the lowest cost. It helps smooth the flow of activities from the patient's presentation of symptoms to doctors' orders to the timely delivery of appropriate treatment. Healthcare service production management can serve a number of purposes, all of which are related to the type of patient and patient requirements determined by doctors' orders. In the standardization of production management, the methods of Lean production create visual checkpoints throughout the service production process for all aspects of the management function so that communication is immediate and universal. Visual displays and controls, mistake-proofing, and quick setup methods continually decrease work-in-process inventory and defects. Clinicians and support staff become their own inspectors of both the process and the technical standards.

Standards are the foundation of continuous improvement. Without them, you cannot focus or measure your improvements. By the time you have implemented a new work area layout, quick setup, and standard work, everyone should have embraced a culture of continuous improvement. Standards and standard work, as we have shown throughout this book, are not static or unchanging. In fact, they are the basis from which improvement changes can be analyzed, tested, and then adopted systematically by everyone. They are the content of training efforts—you train people to adhere to both technical and process standards. Standard work, when implemented, creates an even workload for every clinician and staff member, so that no one works too little or too much, idle time is reduced, bottlenecks are eliminated, and patients no longer wait to be seen, assessed, diagnosed, and treated.

Generally, you will discover that clinicians and support staff resist standardization until they understand what it really means and how it benefits them and the organization. In fact, 100 percent of the time, once standardization is in effect and standard work is in place, creativity, improvement, and job satisfaction increase. Only after working in an environment where standard work is in place do you discover the advantages to each employee that inevitably result.

REFLECTIONS

Now that you have completed this chapter, take five minutes to think about these questions and write down your answers:

1. What did you learn from reading this chapter that stands out as particularly useful or interesting?
2. Do you have any questions about the topics presented in this chapter? If so, what are they?
3. What additional information do you need to understand fully the ideas presented in this chapter?

Chapter 7

Reflection and Conclusions

7.1 REFLECTING ON WHAT YOU HAVE LEARNED

Key Point

An important part of learning is reflecting on what you have learned. Without this step, learning cannot take place effectively because few connections can be made to your existing knowledge and thus little useful information can be fixed in long-term memory. Now that you have come to the end of this book, we would like to ask you to reflect on what you have learned. We suggest you take 10 minutes to write down some quick answers to the following questions:

1. Have you gotten what you wanted to get out of this book?
2. Why or why not?
3. What ideas, tools, and techniques have you learned that will be most useful in healthcare? How will they be useful?
4. What ideas, tools, and techniques have you learned that will be least useful in your own life, at work, or at home? Why aren't they useful?

7.2 APPLYING WHAT YOU HAVE LEARNED

7.2.1 Possibilities for Applying What You Have Learned

The way you decide to apply what you have learned will depend on your situation. If your organization is launching a full-scale Lean (or Six Sigma or Lean-Sigma) transformation program in which standard work will be implemented throughout the organization, you should have many opportunities to apply what you have learned in this book in your own workplace. In this case, you may be included on a team of people who are responsible for implementing the standard work in a certain work area. You may have implementation time structured into your workday and may be responsible for reporting the results of your activities on a regular basis.

Key Point

On the other end of the spectrum, your organization may have no immediate plans to implement Lean healthcare or standard work. In this case, the extent to which you can implement what you have learned will depend on how much control you have over your own schedule, workflow, and work area.

7.2.2 Implementing Standardization and Standard Work in Your Organization

Because standardization and standard work appear to be simple on the surface, some managers mistakenly assume that implementation is also simple. As we have already mentioned, successful standardization requires top management participation. In addition, you need the right organization. Figure 7.1 describes a Kaizen leadership team consisting of the CEO and direct reports, who set overall transformation strategy and monitor progress. The Kaizen promotion office (KPO) is the "command center" for implementation activity and is led by the KPO vice president, who reports directly to the CEO of the organization. The KPO vice president is supported by a KPO director, who is directly responsible to Lean specialists, who are trained and certified in the methods of standardization and standard work as well as many other Lean methods.

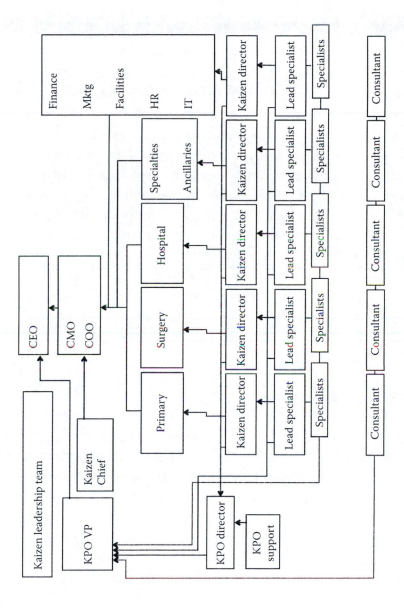

FIGURE 7.1 Kaizen leadership team. (Reprinted with permission. J. Michael Rona and Associates, LLC, doing business as Rona Consulting Group © 2008–2011 ©. All rights reserved. http://www.ronaconsulting.com)

Lean specialists are assigned to the organization's service lines and supporting administrative departments. In addition to Lean specialists, the KPO director is indirectly responsible for trained and certified Kaizen directors, who report directly to their service line and department leaders.

In addition to the right organization, you will need a detailed implementation plan. Figure 7.2 shows how you might plan an implementation focused on Lean healthcare, at the very core of which is standard work. This plan follows the Plan-Do-Check-Act (PDCA) logic we explored in Chapter 4 (see Figures 4.5 and 4.6). In the Plan phase of implementation, senior management is trained thoroughly in Lean techniques and organizes a KPO. In the Do phase of implementation, the KPO deploys standard work throughout the organization's key service lines. In the Check phase, the KPO focuses on adherence to standard work by implementing 5S and visual management. In the Act phase, the KPO focuses on introducing continuous improvement by training everyone in standardized problem-solving methods. The whole purpose of the plan is to deploy standard work, ensure adherence, and promote continuous improvement in all healthcare operations, in all supporting areas (including finance and human resource management), and ultimately in the organization's key suppliers.

7.2.3 Your Personal Action Plan

Key Point

You may or may not be in a management position that permits you to plan or implement standardization or standard work on a grand scale. Whatever your situation, we suggest you create a personal action plan for how you will begin applying the information you have learned from this book. You might start by referring to your own notes about the tools and techniques you think will be most useful to you, then writing down answers to the following questions:

1. What can I implement right now at work that will make my job easier, better, or more efficient?
2. What can I implement at home right now that will make activities there flow more easily or more efficiently?

Plan		Do		Check		Act	
Kaizen Leadership Team	Find your sensei Train and certify the kaizen leadership team in standardization, standard work, and lean thinking	Set up and staff the kaizen promotion office system	Build and deploy a company wide improvement policy	Conduct weekly and monthly progress reviews of value stream process improvement metrics & financial results		Go "beyond budgeting" and focus on the process, not results	Conduct the first annual president's diagnosis using the transformation ruler
Kaizen Promotion Office	Train and certify a core group of senior executives, lead specialists, and kaizen directors in standardization, standard work, and other Lean methods	• Value stream maps • Standard work • Quick setup • Five S	• Visual control • PDCA • Stop the line • Continuous flow	The number of modules expands to incorporate methods aimed at creating pull scheduling and supporting continuous improvement. By the end of this period the client is able to train and certify experts in all relevant Lean tools		• Kanban • Mistake-proofing • Systematic PDCA • Total productive maintenance	• Hoshin kanri • Value stream accounting • Transformation ruler
Service Line Leadership	Conduct time studies and value stream map the operating room, emergency room, inpatient flow, clinics, and ancillary services	Build standard work sheets, standard work combination sheets, percent load charts	Reduce setup times; redesign work flow; implement standard work and promote adherence w/five S	• Promote adherence through visual management • Implement patient safety andon system • Introduce PDCA problem solving documentation • Implement pull scheduling to link ancillary services and doctor referrals with healthcare operations:		Improve continuously by implementing: • Systematic PDCA throughout the organization • Mistake-proofing • Six sigma	
Administrative and Support Leadership				Value stream map administrative operations, including accounting and human resources	Conduct times studies and build percent load charts; introduce Lean accounting practices	Reduce setup times redesign work flow implement standard work and promote adherence w/five S	Improve continuously: • Systematic PDCA • Mistake-proofing
New Services and Facilities				Value stream map new service development process and establish a gated development system w/strict design review	Improve program management: • A3P and the QC matrix • Target costing • Kaizen costing		Improve continuously: • Systematic PDCA • Mistake-proofing
Value Chain Transformation				Reduce number of suppliers based upon performance criteria	Measure quality, cost, & delivery; give feedback to suppliers	Work with suppliers, to eliminate waste, standardize work, and solve problems	Involve key suppliers upstream in the development of new services and facilities

FIGURE 7.2 Transformation road map. (Reprinted with permission. J. Michael Rona and Associates, LLC, doing business as Rona Consulting Group © 2008–2011 ©. All rights reserved. http://www.ronaconsulting.com)

3. How can I involve others at work and at home in the implementation of what I have learned?

When you have answered these questions, we suggest that you commit to completing the things you have written down in a specific period and to making a new plan at the end of that time period.

Key Point

In implementing anything, it is often good to start with something small that you can comfortably finish in the time you have allowed yourself. If the project is too ambitious or time-consuming you can easily get discouraged and give up.

Key Point

In addition, projects you can work on for short periods whenever you get a chance are ideal in the beginning. For example, you might decide to standardize your medication rooms to reduce inadvertent medication errors by laying them out and labeling them identically. Alternatively, you might improve the process of registration, improving both lead time and the quality of information gathered from patients by implementing standard work.

7.3 OPPORTUNITIES FOR FURTHER LEARNING

Here are some ways to learn more about standards and standardized work.

- Find other books or videos on this subject. Several of these are listed in the Appendix.
- If your organization is already implementing the standard work, visit other departments to see how they are using the tools and techniques and standard work.
- Find out how other healthcare organizations have implemented standardization and standard work.
- Consider visiting local manufacturing companies with successful standard work implementations.

CONCLUSIONS

The approach of standardization and standard work is a simple but powerful method for improvement in the healthcare environment. We hope this book has given you a taste of how this method can be helpful and effective for you in your work. Productivity Press and the Rona Consulting Group welcome your stories about how you apply standardization and standard work in your own workplace.

Appendix

FURTHER READING ABOUT THE 5S SYSTEM

The following resources available from Productivity Press will provide you with additional education about various aspects of the five-pillar system.

Productivity Press Development Team, Ed., *5 Pillars of the Visual Workplace* (New York: Productivity Press, 1995)—This is the source-book for *5S for Healthcare*. It includes case studies, numerous illustrations, and detailed information about how to initiate and manage a five-pillar implementation effort in any organization.

M. Greif, *The Visual Factory: Building Participation Through Shared Information* (New York: Productivity Press, 1991)—This book shows how visual management techniques can provide "just-in-time" information to support teamwork and employee participation on the healthcare facility floor.

N. K. Shimbun, Ed., *Visual Control Systems* (New York: Productivity Press, 1995)—This book presents articles and case studies that detail how visual control systems have been implemented in a variety of organizations.

FURTHER READING ABOUT LEAN HEALTHCARE

M. Graban, *Lean Hospitals: Improving Quality, Patient Safety, and Employee Satisfaction* (New York: Productivity Press, 2009)—This book explains why and how Lean can be used to improve quality, safety, and morale in a healthcare setting. Graban highlights the benefits of Lean methods and explains how Lean manufacturing staples such as value stream mapping can help hospital personnel identify and eliminate waste, effectively preventing delays for patients, reducing wasted motion for caregivers, and improving quality of care.

N. Grunden, *The Pittsburgh Way: Improving Patient Care Using Toyota Based Methods* (New York: Productivity Press, 2008)—This book provides a hopeful look at how principles borrowed from industry can be applied to make healthcare safer and, in doing so, make it more efficient and less costly. The book is a compilation of case studies from units in different hospitals around the Pittsburgh region that applied industrial principles successfully, making patients safer and employees more satisfied.

J. C. Bauer and M. Hagland, *Paradox and Imperatives in Health Care: How Efficiency, Effectiveness, and E-Transformation Can Conquer Waste and Optimize Quality* (New York: Productivity Press, 2008)—This book explains why providers must draw upon internal resources to increase net revenue and provide the quality of care that payers and consumers are demanding. Through numerous case studies, the authors show how pioneering health care organizations are using performance improvement tools—including Lean management, Six Sigma, and the Toyota Production System—to produce excellent services as inexpensively as possible.

USEFUL WEBSITES

http://www.leanblog.org/ A blog founded by author Mark Graban about Lean in factories, hospitals, and the world around us.

John Grout's Mistake Proofing Center. http://www.mistakeproofing.com Shingo Prize-winner John Grout's collection of three websites devoted to poka-yoke (mistake proofing), a key technique for 5S and Lean operations generally. An entire website within the center is devoted to healthcare applications of mistake proofing.

www.ronaconsulting.com The official website of Series Editor, Thomas L. Jackson and his partners at the Rona Consulting Group.

www.productivitypress.com The website of Productivity Press, where you may order the books mentioned previously, among many others about Lean manufacturing, total quality management, and total productive maintenance.

Index